Too Soon Old,
Too Late Smart

Also by Gordon Livingston

Only Spring: On Mourning the Death of My Son

Too Soon Old, Too Late Smart

*Thirty True Things
You Need to Know Now*

Gordon Livingston, M.D.

FOREWORD BY ELIZABETH EDWARDS

MARLOWE & COMPANY
NEW YORK

TOO SOON OLD, TOO LATE SMART: *Thirty True Things You Need to Know Now*
Copyright © 2004 by Gordon Livingston
Foreword copyright © 2004 by Elizabeth Edwards

Published by
Marlowe & Company
An Imprint of Avalon Publishing Group Incorporated
245 West 17th Street • 11th Floor
New York, NY 10011-5300

A V A L O N

Grateful acknowledgment is made to the following for permission to reprint previously published material: United Artists/EMI, for the excerpt on page 74 from Tom Paxton's "The Last Thing On My Mind" (© 1964 (Renewed) United Artists Music Co. Inc. All Rights Reserved. Used by Permission. WARNER BROS. PUBLICATIONS U.S. INC., Miami, FL. 33014); and Grove/Atlantic, for the excerpt on page 168 from Raymond Carver's "Late Fragment," from *A New Path to the Waterfall* (Copyright © 1989 by the estate of Raymond Carver. Used by permission of Grove/Atlantic, Inc.)

Library of Congress Cataloging-in-Publication Data
Livingston, Gordon.
Too soon old, too late smart: thirty true things you need to know now / by Gordon Livingston.
p. cm.
ISBN 1-56924-419-7
1. Conduct of life. I. Title.
BJ1581.2.L58 2004
158--dc22
2004057910

9 8 7

Designed by Maria Elias

Printed in the United States of America
Distributed by Publishers Group West

To my patients
Who taught me most of what is in this book.

And to Clare
Who, beyond all reason, chose to love me.

Contents

Foreword
By Elizabeth Edwards

For the past eight years, Gordon Livingston has been one of the most important people in my life—and yet I have met him only once. Neither of us is young, but we are the beneficiaries of the communication mode of the young: we met on the Internet, in an online community of bereaved parents. He and a handful of others were just what I needed when my child died, people who truly understood the chasm into which we were all falling, trying—sometimes halfheartedly—to grab hold and stop the fall.

There are no words to explain what Gordon's steady eloquence meant in those days. It was a hard truth, unfathomable even to those of us mid-chasm, that Gordon had made this fall twice. I was blessed that I was able to grab hold of Gordon Livingston and his unapologetic directness and his embracing compassion. And as sure as his words were, Gordon did not preach or judge: he illuminated where I stood so I could better see myself and the world around me, and then he took that light and held it out so I could see the footholds and ledges I would need to reclaim a productive life.

What the years have taught me about Gordon is that it doesn't matter whether the fall is into the deep chasm we shared or more like Alice's fall into Wonderland—"I am too small, I am too big, nothing is what it should be"—Gordon's sensible voice expresses a wisdom greater even than what his extraordinary life has provided. The essays in this book give every reader the window view that I have been fortunate enough to sit near for the past eight years. It is a book for which we can all reach when we need that thoughtful voice, just as I often reach for the folder in my desk marked "Gordon"—a collection of his e-mails and posts—when I need a voice that is at once stern and reassuring, hopeful but unwilling to proffer any guarantees. For he knows, as well as anyone could, that life will have its way with us and that all we can hope to do is to keep ourselves in alignment for the bumpy ride. He once wrote to me: "All I know is what I feel and what I hope." It was classic understatement by Gordon; he seems to know also what I feel and hope and what you feel and hope, and which of those feelings are honest and which of those hopes are attainable. Gordon, who is also a pilot, continued, "I hope that when the airspeed indicator reaches sixty that I can pull back on the yoke and the thing will fly. I've had the physics explained to me a hundred times. Bernoulli was fortuitously correct. But it still seems like a miracle." And those words ring true because, despite his experience, Gordon has somehow managed to retain the faith of the innocent, the uninitiated.

As I read his essays, I was reminded of a trailer for a self-improvement television series: "Your friends won't tell you . . . but we're not your friends and we will." Well, maybe that's what real friends do: say the hard things that we need to know if we are to be stronger, better, more generous, more courageous, kinder. It might not always be comfortable to hear what Gordon has to say. He will push you out of the easy chair in which you expected to sit and watch television until the lights go out—for your own good, of course. At the same time that he warns us how little we control, he reminds us that we are never stripped of all our choices. Like a wise parent, he shoves us in the right direction . . . with a velvet-gloved hand.

Gordon and I come from different worlds, and on many things we have different perspectives. Even when we disagree, as we do on some things—even some matters covered in these essays—I appreciate that he has expressed so cogently his argument without the rancor and incivility that has come to mark so much of contemporary dialogue. And—to my chagrin when we disagree—he makes the best possible argument for his side.

I was so pleased to be given the opportunity to write this foreword, to introduce Gordon Livingston to those who don't yet know his grace. And most of all, I'm grateful for the chance to repeat to Gordon the words of his son Lucas, who at six was awaiting death as the bone marrow Gordon had donated failed to work the medical magic they both deserved: "I love your voice."

A passionate advocate for children and an accomplished attorney, **ELIZABETH EDWARDS** *is active in a variety of community and charitable efforts, including the March of Dimes, University of North Carolina Board of Visitors, Books for Kids, and the Wade Edwards Foundation. She is married to John Edwards, with whom she is the proud parent of four children: Wade, who died in 1996, Cate, Emma Claire, and Jack.*

Too Soon Old,
Too Late Smart

If the map doesn't agree with the ground,
the map is wrong.

Once, a long time ago, I was a young lieutenant in the 82nd Airborne Division, trying to orient myself on a field problem at Fort Bragg, North Carolina. As I stood studying a map, my platoon sergeant, a veteran of many junior officers, approached. "You figure out where we are, lieutenant?" he asked. "Well, the map says there should be a hill over there, but I don't see it," I replied. "Sir," he said, "if the map don't agree with the ground, then the map is wrong." Even at the time, I knew I had just heard a pro-found truth.

Over the many years I have spent listening to people's sto-ries, especially all the ways in which things can go awry, I have learned that our passage through life consists of an effort to get the maps in our heads to conform to the ground on which we walk. Ideally, this process takes place as we grow. Our parents teach us, primarily by example, what they have learned. Unfor-tunately, we are seldom wholly receptive to these lessons. And often, our parents' lives suggest to us that they have little useful to convey, so that much of what we know comes to us through the frequently painful process of trial and error.

To single out an important life task about which most of us could use some instruction, we might look at choosing (and keeping) a mate. The fact that upward of half of all mar-riages end in divorce indicates that collectively we are not very good at this task. When we look at our parents' relation-ship(s), we are usually not reassured. I find few people who would be satisfied with what they have seen in their families of origin, even when their parents' marriages have endured for decades. More often, those whose parents are still together describe them as living a boring or conflicted coexis-tence that makes economic sense but lacks anything one could describe as excitement or emotional satisfaction.

Perhaps predicting what someone will be like (and how much we will like them) in five years, much less fifty, is impossible, and we must accept that society is moving toward a kind of serial monogamy, an acknowledgment that people change over time and that it is naive to expect the love of our youth to endure. The problem is that serial monogamy is not a very good model for child rearing, since it does not provide the stability and security that children need in order to begin to construct their maps of how the world works.

So what is it exactly that we need to know to decide if someone is a suitable candidate for a lifetime commitment? Perhaps one way to approach this screening process is to learn more about who is evidently *not* suitable. To make this judgment, one needs to know something about personality.

We are accustomed to thinking about character in the most superficial ways. "He has a lot of personality" is usually a statement about how engaging or entertaining someone is. In fact, the formal definition of personality includes our habitual ways of thinking, feeling, and relating to others. Most of us understand that people differ in certain characteristics, such as introversion, fondness for detail, tolerance for boredom, willingness to be helpful, determination, and a host of other personal qualities. What most people fail to realize, however, is that the qualities we value—kindness, tolerance, capacity for commitment—are not randomly distributed. They tend to exist as constellations of "traits" that are recognizable and reasonably stable over time.

Likewise, those attributes of character that are less desirable—impulsivity, self-centeredness, quickness to anger—often cluster in discernible ways. Much of our difficulty in developing and sustaining personal relationships resides in our failure to recognize, in ourselves as well as in others, those personality characteristics that make someone a poor candidate for a committed relationship.

The psychiatric profession has taken the trouble to categorize personality disorders. I often think that this section of the diagnostic manual ought to be titled "People to avoid." The many labels contained herein—histrionic, narcissistic, dependent, borderline, and so on—form a catalogue of unpleasant persons: suspicious, selfish, unpredictable, exploitative. These are the people your mother warned you about. (Unfortunately, sometimes they are your mother.) They seldom exist in the unalloyed form suggested by the statistical manual, but knowing something about how to recognize them would save a lot of heartbreak.

What would be equally useful, I think, would be a manual of virtuous character traits that describes qualities to nurture in ourselves and to seek in our friends and lovers. At the top of the list would be *kindness*, a willingness to give of oneself to another. This most desirable of virtues governs all the others, including a capacity for empathy and love. Like other forms of art, we may find it hard to define, but when we are in its presence, we feel it.

This is the map we wish to construct in our heads: a reliable guide that allows us to avoid those who are not worthy of our time and trust and to embrace those who are. The best indications that our always-tentative maps are faulty include feelings of sadness, anger, betrayal, surprise, and disorientation. It is when these feelings surface that we need to think about our mental instrument of navigation and how to correct it, so that we do not fall into the repetitive patterns of those who waste the learning that is the only consolation for our painful experience.

2

We are what we do.

People often come to me asking for medication. They are tired of their sad mood, fatigue, and loss of interest in things that previously gave them pleasure. They are having trouble sleeping or they sleep all the time; their appetites are absent or excessive. They are irritable and their memories are shot. Often they wish they were dead. They have trouble remembering what it is to be happy.

I listen to their stories. Each one is, of course, different, but there are certain recurrent themes: Others in their families have lived similarly discouraged lives. The relationships in which they now find themselves are either full of conflict or "low temperature," with little passion or intimacy. Their days are routine: unsatisfying jobs, few friends, lots of boredom. They feel cut off from the pleasures enjoyed by others.

Here is what I tell them: *The good news is that we have effective treatments for the symptoms of depression; the bad news is that medication will not make you happy. Happiness is not simply the absence of despair. It is an affirmative state in which our lives have both meaning and pleasure.*

So medication alone is seldom enough. People also need to look at the way they are living with an eye to change. We are always talking about what we want, what we intend. These are dreams and wishes and are of little value in changing our mood. We are not what we think, or what we say, or how we feel. *We are what we do.* Conversely, in judging other people we need to pay attention not to what they promise but to how they behave. This simple rule could prevent much of the pain and misunderstanding that infect human relationships. "When all is said and done, more is said than done." We are drowning in words, many of which turn out to be lies we tell ourselves or others. How many times do we have to feel betrayed and surprised at the disconnect between people's words and their actions before we learn to pay more attention to the latter than the former? Most of the heartbreak that life contains is a result of ignoring the reality that *past behavior is the most reliable predictor of future behavior*.

Woody Allen famously said that "Eighty percent of life is showing up." We demonstrate courage in the numberless small ways in which we meet our obligations or reach out to try the new things that might improve our lives. Many of us are afraid of risk and prefer the bland, the predictable, and the repetitive. This explains the overwhelming sense of boredom that is a defining characteristic of our age. The frantic attempts to overcome this *ennui* take the form of a thirst for entertainment and stimulation that is, in the end, devoid of meaning. It is the answer to the question "Why?" that weighs most heavily upon us. Why are we here? Why do we choose the lives we do? Why bother? The despairing answer is contained in a popular bumper sticker: "Whatever."

In general we get, not what we deserve, but what we expect. Ask a successful hitter in baseball about what he thinks will happen when he steps to the plate and you will hear something like, "I'm taking that thing downtown!" If you point out that the best hitters in the game make an out two of three times they bat, any good player will say, "Yeah, but this is my time."

The three components of happiness are something to do, someone to love, and something to look forward to. Think about it. If we have useful work, sustaining relationships, and the promise of pleasure, it is hard to be unhappy. I use the term "work" to encompass any activity, paid or unpaid, that gives us a feeling of personal significance. If we have a compelling avocation that lends meaning to our lives, that is our work. It is a tribute to the diversity of human life that people can find pleasure and meaning in pursuing mediocrity on the golf course or at the bridge table. Think about the traffic problems if we all liked the same thing.

Much is made of the presumed difficulty in defining "love." Because the basis for the feeling itself is mysterious (Why do I love this person and not someone else?), it is assumed that words cannot encompass what it means to love another. How about this definition? *We love someone when the importance of his or her needs and desires rises to the level of our own*. In the best of cases, of course, our concern for the welfare of another *exceeds*, or becomes indistinguishable from, what we want for ourselves. An operational question I use to help people determine if they really love someone is, "Would you take a bullet for this person?" This may seem an extreme standard, since few of us are required to confront such a sacrifice and none of us can say with certainty what we would do if our desire for self-preservation collided with our love for another. But just imagining the situation can clarify the nature of our attachments.

The number of people we would consider sacrificing ourselves to save is very limited: our children, certainly; our spouse or other "loved one," maybe. But if we cannot contemplate this gift, how can we pretend that we love them? More commonly, feelings of love or the lack of it are noticeable in all the mundane ways we show that someone matters to us, especially in the amount and quality of the time we are willing to give them.

The point is that love is demonstrated behaviorally. Once again we define who we are and who and what we care about, not by what we promise, but by what we do. I constantly redirect people's attention to this. We are a verbal species, much given to the use of words to explain—and deceive. The worst deceptions, of course, are those we practice on ourselves. What we choose to believe is closely related to deeply felt needs—for example, the dream we all carry around inside us of perfect love, unqualified acceptance of the sort available only from a good mother. This desire makes us vulnerable to the worst forms of self-deception and disillusionment, an indulgence of the hope that we have at last found the person who will endlessly love us exactly as we are.

When, therefore, someone purports to do so and says the words we so long to hear, it is not surprising that we might choose to ignore incongruent behaviors. When I hear someone say, "He does inconsiderate things, but I know he loves me," I usually ask if it is possible to intentionally hurt someone we love. Would we do such a thing to ourselves? Can we love the truck that runs us over?

The other thing that true love requires of us is the courage to become totally vulnerable to another. The risks are obvious. Who has not had their heart lacerated by a mistake in judging the person to whom we gave this trust? Such wounds are the basis for much of the cynicism about love that pervades our relationships and produces the competitive games that frustrate our efforts to have faith in each other.

Often people alternate between the extremes of loneliness and self-deception. Somewhere in the middle lies our best chance at happiness. Finally, we are entitled to receive only that which we are prepared to give. This is why there is truth to the adage that we all get the marriage partners we deserve, and why most of our dissatisfactions with others reflect limitations in ourselves.

It is difficult to remove by logic an idea not placed there by logic in the first place.

In my experience, therapists waste a lot of time trying to convince people to relinquish behaviors that make no sense, that are maladaptive, that appear "illogical." For example, a man returns home from work and the first thing out of his mouth is, "This place is a mess." His children scatter and his wife, who just got home from *her* work and picking the kids up from day care, is angry. Their evening is off to a bad start. Hearing this story, the therapist points out that it is a predictably bad idea to criticize a tired wife at the end of a long day. All agree that this is a correct observation, but the behavior doesn't change, or the criticism simply migrates to another issue. Both people remain unhappy with each other and conflict between them continues.

What's going on here? Why do people not seem to understand that criticism begets anger and unhappiness? There is no single answer to this question, of course, but confronting deeply held, habitual feelings and attitudes with logic seldom works. The things we do, the prejudices that we hold, and the repetitive conflicts that afflict our lives are seldom the products of rational thought. In fact, *we operate in the world mostly on autopilot*, doing the same things today that didn't work yesterday. One would think that a process of learning or maturation would cause us to alter our behavior in response to unpleasant consequences. Anyone who has watched an average golfer play knows that this is not true.

In fact, it sometimes seems that we are so trapped in ineffectual life patterns that we are playing out the old military adage: *If it doesn't work, double it.* The motivations and habit patterns that underlie most of our behavior are seldom logical; we are much more often driven by impulses, preconceptions, and emotions of which we are only dimly aware.

In the example above, the man returning home is subject

to feelings of discontent evoked by his unsatisfying job or lengthy commute. He longs for some control over his life that proves maddeningly elusive. He enters his home in the hope of refuge, but is confronted only by more obligation and disorder. This is not the life he imagined. So who is responsible?

If most of our behavior is driven by our feelings, however unclear they may be, it follows that to change ourselves we must be able to identify our emotional needs and find ways of satisfying them that do not offend those upon whom our happiness depends. If we wish, as most of us do, to be treated with kindness and forbearance, we need to cultivate those qualities in ourselves. Whenever I talk with couples in conflict, it is striking how similar are their desires: to be respected, to be listened to, to feel that they are the center of their partner's life. What else could we possibly want in a relationship? It is what people mean when they speak of love.

To say that one must give to receive, that we reap as we sow, is to mouth platitudes. Yet what could be truer? Why then is it so difficult to do? Like most explanations of why we act as we do, the answer lies in our past experience.

As children we are entitled to the unconditional love of our parents. But few of the people I talk to feel as though they received it. On the contrary, most childhood memories are freighted with the sense of an unspoken obligation to "make my parents proud"—by succeeding in school, staying out of trouble, making a suitable marriage, and producing grandchildren. Many are the ways that parents instill a sense of obligation in their children. By accepting life and nurturance a child apparently incurs a debt that can be repaid only by meeting parental expectations.

Much is made of the burdens of parenthood. Starting with the pain of childbirth, the loss of sleep with infancy, the endless driving required by organized activities, the stress of adolescent conflict, culminating in the expense of college—each stage of upbringing is a frequent source of parental complaint suggesting a kind of martyrdom. Is it any surprise that there should be some feeling of reciprocal obligation on the part of children?

This question, "What do I owe my parents?" frequently distorts people's lives well into, and sometimes throughout, adulthood. *In fact, our children owe us nothing.* It was our decision to bring them into the world. If we loved them and provided for their needs it was our task as parents, not some selfless act. We knew from the beginning that we were raising them to leave us and it was always our obligation to help them do this unburdened by a sense of unending gratitude or perpetual debt.

Well-functioning families are good at letting their children go. Poorly functioning families tend to hold on to them. When I encounter homes where children continue to live, often unhappily, long into adulthood, I have the feeling that the same conflicts and separation anxieties are being worked on over and over but never resolved. The shared fantasy appears to be that "we'll keep at this until we get it right." Sometimes, it never happens. I know of families with young adults in their 20's and 30's in which the parents still lie awake until the "kids" are home. Where arguments over chores and mealtimes reflect a longing for the past and a fear of an independent future. There is a kind of shared commitment to not changing the family. The young people trade their chance at autonomous lives in exchange for the security of a familiar, childlike existence that serves to reassure their parents that they need not relinquish the responsibilities on which their sense of themselves depends.

In these families the roles are familiar and well-defined and one has the impression of watching a well-rehearsed play in which each of the players has become so practiced that the idea of closing down the production and moving on is extremely anxiety-provoking.

Finally, when struggling to overcome maladaptive behaviors by the use of logic, one is often confronted with the fact that *some ignorance is invincible*. People can become so wedded to their particular view of how things should work that they ignore all evidence that suggests that change is necessary.

The statute of limitations has expired
on most of our childhood traumas.

The stories of our lives, far from being fixed narratives, are under constant revision. The slender threads of causality are rewoven and reinterpreted as we attempt to explain to ourselves and others how we became the people we are. As I listen to these tales of the past, I am impressed by the ways in which people connect the things they experienced as children to who they are today.

So what do we owe our personal histories? Certainly we

are shaped by them and must learn from them if we are to avoid the repetitious mistakes that make us feel trapped in a long-running drama of our own authorship. This is why in the initial stages of psychotherapy it is important to listen to the patient's story uncritically. Contained in those memories are not just the events, but also the meaning they have for that particular person. Since the story is being told by someone who is anxious, depressed, or otherwise dissatisfied with his or her existence, one is likely to hear about grievances and traumas that are presumably in some way connected to current unhappiness.

Every adult American has been sufficiently exposed to pop psychology that he or she is inclined to connect past difficulties to present symptoms. Because acceptance of responsibility for what we do and how we feel requires an act of will, it is natural to blame people in our pasts, especially parents, for not doing a better job.

If there *has* been serious physical, sexual, or psychological trauma it is important to acknowledge and process this. No child escapes unscathed from parental abuse or neglect. What is important is to go about this examination sympathetically, in a way that emphasizes learning but rejects the assumption that even the most awful experiences define our lives forever.

Change is the essence of life. It is the goal of all psychotherapeutic conversation. In order for the process to proceed, however, it must move beyond simple complaint. People often ask me why I don't get bored endlessly listening to patients "whine" about their lives. The answer, of course, is that complaining about how one feels, or about repetitive behaviors that produce familiar and unhappy results, is just the beginning of a process. My favorite therapeutic question is "What's next?" (In an act of consummate subtlety I have a screen saver on my desktop computer, visible to patients, with these words scrolling.)

The question implies both a willingness to change and the power to do so. It bypasses the self-pity implied in clinging to past traumas and recognizes the importance of leveraging goal-oriented conversation, insight, and a therapeutic relationship into changes in behavior.

I don't give much direct advice in therapy—not out of modesty or as a "trick" to get patients to come up with their own solutions to problems, but because most of the time I don't have a clear idea of what people need to do to make themselves better. I am, however, able to sit with them while they figure it out. My job is to hold them to the task, point out connections I think I see between past and present, wonder about underlying motives, and express confidence in their ability to come up with solutions that fit their lives.

A kind of training takes place. People often come into therapy hoping that I will be a source of sage direction on what they need to do. After all, we go to doctors to get prescriptions. We are trained to expect quick solutions. Feeling bad? Take this. The idea that we have to sit and talk about the problems we face and the things we have tried that have failed implies a slow and unwieldy process that has at its core an uncomfortable assumption: *We are responsible for most of what happens to us.*

There is a narrow line that a therapist must walk here. All of us have endured events and losses about which we had no choice. These include the families into which we were born, the way we were treated as children, the deaths and divorces of those close to us. It is not hard to make a case that we have been adversely affected by events and people outside our control.

Attempts by a therapist to reorient the conversation to future choices may be perceived by the patient as unfair and judgmental. Here is where the importance of the therapeutic alliance is greatest. The patient must be convinced that the therapist is on his or her side.

Therapy, properly done, is a combination of confessional,

re-parenting, and mentoring experiences. There is no perfect therapist for all who seek help. Each person has individual needs that cause them to "fit" well or poorly with a given therapist. In addition, the therapist brings his or her life experience, prejudices, and philosophy of change to the process. Often the attempt to connect is futile—occasionally even harmful. Just as with any other human relationship, what works is frequently hard to define or predict.

The qualities of a good therapist mirror those of a good parent: patience, empathy, capacity for affection, and an ability to listen nonjudgmentally. That said, just as parents react differently to different children, so, too, do therapists do a better job with certain patients. What all of us hesitate to admit is that we tend to be more helpful to people who are like us. This seldom-acknowledged prejudice makes logical sense. None of us would be very effective therapists if we were dropped in a foreign country, even if we spoke the language. The subtle combination of cultural mores and expectations would escape us. So, too, within our own society, people live very different lives depending on, for example, their race or social standing. It is arrogant to assume that any of us can work equally well with everyone.

When someone first comes to me for help, one of the things I ask myself as I begin to know him or her is whether I like, or will come to like, this person. If I find myself bored or offended by a patient's story, I know it is time to gently suggest that he or she might work better with someone else. For example, I find a sense of learned helplessness, if it seems intractable, to be hard to work with. If I find that I am providing most of the energy and optimism, or if I am losing hope for change, it is time to stop. If the person I'm seeing reminds me too closely of one of my own parents, of a person with whom I have had conflict, or of a girl who rejected me in adolescence, I know I am in dangerous territory.

Finally, if the person I'm talking to appears wedded determinedly to the past and unwilling to contemplate a better future, I grow impatient. It is misplaced kindness to offer *only* sympathy, even where it is clearly justified. It is *hope* that I'm really selling. If, after extended effort, I cannot persuade someone to buy, I am wasting both our time by continuing.

*Any relationship is under the control
of the person who cares the least.*

Marriages that come to my attention are on life support. Their common theme is that they have become power struggles; in fact, most appear to have been so from the beginning. The issues over which the contest is fought are familiar—money, children, sex—but the underlying causes are usually diminished self-respect and unmet expectations.

Our attempts to find a partner center upon the concept of romantic love, an earthly paradise (or shared delusion) that is the basis for most of the stories we consume about what it means to achieve happiness. The ways in which people come together and choose each other place a great emphasis on the potent combination of sexual attraction and a sort of enlightened self-interest that evaluates the other person on a series of qualities and achievements: education, earning potential, shared interests, trustworthiness, and philosophy of life. Each person's assessment of a prospective mate using these standards creates a certain set of expectations. It is the failure of these expectations over time that causes relationships to dissolve.

If this formulation appears to be overly analytical and to ignore the mysterious process of "falling in love," that is because in my experience the "chemistry" that causes us to choose one person over all other possibilities can be seen in retrospect as a combination of readiness, lust, and hope rather than an indefinable but powerful union of two souls. I would be more ready to believe in the latter if there was more evidence of its persistence over time.

Among the most ominous, and revealing, developments in modern marriage has been the increasing popularity of prenuptial agreements. Once the province of the very wealthy, these contracts have become common among people who are entering into marriage after they have accumulated assets that they are reluctant to share with their partner.

The reasons for protecting what you bring into the marriage sound perfectly valid on the surface. Often each party has children to whom they want to direct their inheritance. Most have already experienced a divorce that has been expensive both financially and emotionally and are aware of statistics that show that second (or third) marriages have an even higher failure rate than first marriages.

Nevertheless, it is discouraging to see a couple about to join their lives acting like purchasers of used cars. We require contracts from people we do not trust; they protect us against those we fear will take advantage of us. To require such an agreement from someone we purport to love reflects a deeply cynical view of the relationship, amounting to a prediction of failure that, like most expectations, is often realized.

The law has been slowly evolving on this point so that "irreconcilable differences" and "no-fault divorce" have replaced the more traditional grounds that were heretofore required to end a marriage. Nevertheless, the need to find reasons for separation often results in a climate of blame in which each person tries to seize the moral high ground—with especially unhappy results for any children involved.

As marriages enter the long slide toward alienation, it is seldom a symmetrical process. One party typically feels and expresses less affection and respect than the other. This appears to be a bid to seize control of the relationship. That this effort has been successful can be seen when one spouse has a greater investment in reconciliation and is much more upset at the prospect of ending the marriage. When I point out to people that much of the distress they are feeling is not shared by their partner and that this is the source of their feeling "out of control," they are usually quick to recognize their predicament. *While it takes two people to create a relationship, it takes only one to end it.*

When I read wedding announcements and look at the smiling pictures of couples newly betrothed, I understand that no one is saying to them, "You know that the chances of this marriage enduring are no better than fifty-fifty. What makes you think that you will win the coin flip?" Such a question would be unthinkable for people with stars in their eyes, so it will not be asked. The ground for disappointment and betrayal is prepared. An act of supreme optimism, courage, or foolishness, depending on your point of view, is encouraged to pursue its hopeful course, and the Ghost of Christmas Future is silent.

Feelings follow behavior.

When people come to a therapist for help, they are seeking to change the way they feel. Whether they struggle with the pervasive sadness of depression or the debilitating constraints of anxiety, they want relief, a return to normalcy. Unwanted emotions are interfering with important areas of functioning in their lives. Often their ability to meet their responsibilities at work and their enjoyment of those they love have been compromised. They suffer from serious deficits in their capacity for pleasure; their lives have an unremitting seriousness; they have lost their capacity to laugh.

Most people know what is good for them, know what will make them feel better: exercise, hobbies, time with those they care about. They do not avoid these things because of ignorance of their value, but because they are no longer "motivated" to do them. They are waiting until they feel better. Frequently, it's a long wait.

As much as we try, *we do not control how we feel or what we think.* Efforts to do so are uniformly frustrating as we struggle against unwanted thoughts and emotions in ways that only exacerbate them. Fortunately, our lives have taught us that certain behaviors predictably bring us pleasure and satisfaction. With this knowledge we are given the opportunity to break the stalemate caused by inaction and its associated feelings of meaninglessness and despair. When people tell me that they feel helpless and unmotivated, I point out that they were able to get out of bed, dress themselves, and drive in to see me. If they can do that, other actions that will make them feel better are obviously possible.

If they say, correctly, that doing things they do not feel like doing is difficult, I acknowledge this and ask if "difficult" means the same thing to them as "impossible." Soon we are talking about things like courage and determination. People seldom associate these virtues with psychotherapy; in fact, they are requirements for any substantial change in the way we live. To ask people to be brave is to expect them to think of their lives in a new way.

But any change requires that we try new things, risking always the possibility that we might fail. Another question I often ask patients is, "What are you saving yourself for?" In our efforts to be compassionate and helpful to those suffering from anxiety and depression and to destigmatize these conditions, we have equated them to physical illness requiring medication. It is true that the current crop of antidepressants has proven remarkably effective. The downside to the medical approach is that illness in this society is a responsibility-relieving state. The ill are infantilized, sometimes placed in hospital beds, told to take it easy and allow their medicine to work. The implication is that they have temporarily and through no fault of their own lost control of their lives and now have to assume a passive role and give themselves, with the aid of medical science, a chance to heal. While this process is going on, little is expected of them. Unfortunately, this approach can be counterproductive.

It is easy to see how we got into this bind. In fact, it is clear that a predisposition to many emotional disorders does have a genetic basis. Alcoholism, for example, runs in families and produces catastrophic changes in our bodies that can kill us if we continue to drink. Is it therefore, as the billboards would have it, *a disease* in the same sense that pneumonia and diabetes are diseases? If so, is it fair to expect those whose drinking is out of control to do anything about this, or are they helpless in the face of their illness?

The successful treatment of alcoholism and other addictions has demonstrated that those who suffer from them *are* obligated to DO something, namely to refuse to drink or use other substances in order to control their condition. The most effective means to this end is through the group support provided by Alcoholics Anonymous or Narcotics Anonymous, organizations with the core belief that each addict has a responsibility to stop using that cannot be dodged, rationalized, or shifted to another person.

Those who are living with a drinking alcoholic are frequently placed in a bind by the disease model. If their loved one suffers from an illness, how fair is it to insist on abstinence? The same goes for other emotional disorders. It is clear, for example, that people who suffer the debilitating mood swings that characterize bipolar disorder are suffering from an organic illness. Is it reasonable then to insist that they take the mood-stabilizing medication that is the treatment for this condition, or must we accept as inevitable the lapses in judgment that are one of the most prominent symptoms of the illness?

What of those who suffer from a personality disorder characterized by maladaptive and well-ingrained patterns of behavior that cause people to be impulsive, dishonest, or emotionally labile? Are these conditions also illnesses deserving of the indulgence we reserve for those who cannot help themselves?

There are a variety of behavioral problems that have at their core the same relief from responsibility that character- izes physical illness. Oddly, they tend to be known by their initials, MPD, BPD, ADD, and so on. The classic condition in this regard has been Multiple Personality Disorder, now, in the ever-migrating world of psychiatric diagnoses, called DID, Dissociative Identity Disorder (or the Devil in Disguise). This condition, popularized in movies like *The Three Faces of Eve* and *Carrie*, is characterized by the presence of two or more distinct personalities that alternately take control of a person's behavior. MPD, now thankfully less in vogue than it was sev- eral years ago, continues to have adherents in spite of the fact that it is almost certainly a therapist-induced state in highly suggestible people. As a reliever of responsibility, it has been promulgated as a legal defense and generally given the short shrift it deserves by juries whose common sense outweighed the "experts" dragged in to support it.

A currently more common example of a diagnostic fad is adult Attention Deficit Disorder (ADD). Disorganized, daydreaming procrastinators now have a medical explanation for their inattention AND an effective treatment: stimulant drugs. People uniformly report that their spirits are better and that they get more done when taking an amphetamine. To which I can only reply, "Me, too."

The point is, in an effort to destigmatize genuine mental illness (severe depression, schizophrenia, bipolar disorder), we have created a plethora of diagnoses that are really just descriptions of certain patterns of behavior. That some of these appear to respond to one sort of psychotropic drug or another just confirms our belief that they are "diseases." For example, it has long been observed that women who are victims of spousal abuse are dependent people who have trouble separating themselves from their abuser. By labeling this "Battered Wife Syndrome" we imply that they lack a capacity to change their situation and should be held to a different standard of responsibility for their choices than other people.

It is not hard to see the insult embedded in such an assumption. It implies the indulgence we extend to children and the physically disabled. Indeed, we have created a whole system by which people can be certified by the government as emotionally disabled and eligible for welfare just as if they were confined to a wheelchair. This makes sense for those suffering from true mental illness who are out of contact with reality or in the grip of uncontrollable swings in mood. When applied to people who abuse food, alcohol, or other substances, or who simply require medication to control their anxiety, the term "disabled" removes not only any sense of responsibility for overcoming one's problems, it damages irrevocably the self-respect that comes with the sense of being a free person on the earth, able to struggle with and overcome adversity.

Like other forms of welfare, compensating people who feel helpless validates this emotion and insures that it persists, while creating a powerful incentive to surrender one's autonomy and sense of competence. In other words, such a system undermines the self-esteem of those it purports to help and constitutes a self-fulfilling affirmation of dependency and hopelessness. All you need to play this particular game is a note from your doctor and the patience to wait while a giant bureaucracy certifies you as disabled. Lawyers, needless to say, are available to speed up the process.

It is our determination to overcome fear and discouragement that constitutes the only effective antidote to the sense of powerlessness over unwanted feelings. Some people are obviously more genetically predisposed to suffer these discomforts than others. While medication can provide crucial, sometimes life-saving relief, people also have an obligation to alter their behavior in ways that allow them to exert greater control over their lives.

The role of victim is generally accompanied by a sense of shame and self-blame. This is true of those victimized by huge social catastrophes (slavery, the Holocaust) or by individual ordeals (crime, illness). This is why there is a fine line between expressing empathy and solidarity for those who suffer and endorsing a passive dependency.

7

*Be bold, and mighty forces will come
to your aid.*

When I was young I spent some time at war. I went to
Vietnam for a variety of reasons, the most important
of which was to find out if I was brave. I was also depressed at
the time, so perhaps there was a bit of a death wish thrown in.
In any event, I supported the war. We had to stop Commu-
nism somewhere, or so I believed. Some combat experience
also would help my budding career in military medicine.

I was a newly promoted major at the time and so I was

assigned as Regimental Surgeon to the 11th Armored Cavalry Regiment (Blackhorse), a 5,000-man unit operating northwest of Saigon. The commanding officer was George S. Patton III. You may have heard of his father.

I did my best to fit in. I spent a lot of time in helicopters, was shot at some, received a Bronze Star for pulling a couple of enemy soldiers out of a difficult spot. But the more I saw of that war, the less proud I became of my participation in it. What we were doing there was so overwhelmingly destructive to that country and its people that it was absurd to pretend that we were fighting on their behalf. We also didn't show them much respect. To us they were "gooks," or "slopes," or "dinks." I just got tired of it. And the costs to us were astronomical. The number of dead Americans eventually reached 58,000. You can read their names on a black granite wall in Washington.

I remember the moment when I knew we were going to lose the war. Frustrated by our inability to find the elusive Viet Cong, we had developed a top-secret program to locate enemy troop concentrations. It was called a "people sniffer," a device sensitive to the presence of ammonia in urine; it could be hung from a helicopter flying low over the jungle. When a high reading was identified, artillery was directed at the area. One evening in 1968 I attended an end-of-the-day regimental briefing where an infantry captain was describing a sweep through the jungle. He and his men had encountered something they could not explain: buckets of urine hanging from the trees. Patton and his intelligence officer exchanged looks of chagrin as they silently acknowledged that we were firing artillery, at $250 a round, at buckets of urine all over Vietnam. It seems funnier now than it did then.

Anyway, I had had enough. On Easter Sunday 1969, I passed among the guests at a change-of-command ceremony for Colonel Patton and handed everyone copies of something I had written the night before. I called it "The Blackhorse Prayer":

God, our Heavenly Father, hear our prayer. We acknowledge our shortcomings and ask thy help in being better soldiers for thee. Grant us, O Lord, those things we need to do thy work more effectively. Give us this day a gun that will fire ten thousand rounds a second, a napalm that will burn for a week. Help us to bring death and destruction wherever we go, for we do it in thy name and therefore it is meet and just. We thank thee for this war, fully mindful that, while it is not the best of all wars, it is better than no war at all. We remember that Christ said "I came not to send peace, but a sword," and we pledge ourselves in all our works to be like Him. Forget not the least of thy children as they hide from us in the jungles; bring them under our merciful hand that we may end their suffering. In all things, O God, assist us, for we do our noble work in the knowledge that only with thy help can we avoid the catastrophe of peace that threatens us ever. All of which we ask in the name of thy son, George Patton. Amen.

There were some high-ranking people there, including General Creighton Abrams, the commander of U.S. forces in Vietnam. There were also a lot of journalists. One of them asked Patton if that was the official unit prayer.

I was arrested and an investigation was launched to see if I was a candidate for court-martial. They decided against it. It would have been inconvenient to try a West Point graduate who could testify firsthand about war crimes. So they sent me home as "an embarrassment to the command." I subsequently resigned from the Army and worked with many others to end the war. We were not immediately successful. It took four years and 25,000 additional American deaths before the last U.S. soldiers finally left.

Twenty-six years later I went back to Vietnam, accompanied by seventeen members of my old unit as well as my son Michael, whom I had found there as an infant in an orphanage during the war. We visited the sites where we had lived and fought so long ago. Our guides included former North Vietnamese and Viet Cong soldiers who carried with them their own memories of the war. They were friendly and welcoming. It was easier for them, I suppose; they had won. Nearly all traces of our having been there had been obliterated. Our biggest installation at Long Binh was being developed as an industrial park.

Half the current population of Vietnam was not even alive during the war. The young people we met as we revisited the scenes of our struggles must have wondered what we were looking for, not knowing what it was we remembered. We carried the burdens of time and fate and our hearts were weighted with the knowledge of those who could not return and whose stories were lost to all except those who loved them.

As I stood on the site of that 1969 change-of-command ceremony I remembered the anger and the doubt and the fear I felt on that Easter Sunday when, with the help of a prayer, I was reborn.

The perfect is the enemy of the good.

M ost of us devote great amounts of time and energy to efforts to assert control over what happens to us in our uncertain progress through life. We are taught to pursue an elusive form of security, primarily through the acquisition of material goods and the means to obtain them. There is a kind of track that we are put on early in life with the implicit suggestion that, if we "succeed," we will be happy and secure.

The primary means to this end is education. The structured

pursuit of schooling provides a systematic classification of social standing and potential for success, as well as a set of intermediate goals that satisfy our need to reassure ourselves of progress. Each graduation carries with it the promise of enhanced status and economic well-being. Finally, it is hoped, we will have amassed a set of specialized skills that people will pay for and we can accumulate those things that are necessary for full membership in a society that guarantees to its citizens the pursuit of happiness.

We are also taught that it is important to form intimate relationships that satisfy important needs—access to sex, the establishment of a stable economic unit, the ability to parent—and to achieve other objectives involving self-regard and emotional security. The directions we are given by our elders tend to focus on economic success. We are left on our own to discover how to relate to others, particularly those of the opposite sex whose needs and desires, while theoretically complementary to our own, remain frustratingly obscure.

A problem emerges with the concept that in order to control our own lives we must exert control over the lives of others. We are then engaged in a zero-sum game in which we get what we want only at the expense of someone else.

We live in a competitive society. We are forever dividing the world up into winners and losers: Republicans versus

Democrats, good versus evil, our team versus their team. Our capitalist system is founded on competition; our legal system thrives on conflict and the pursuit of self-interest. Is it any wonder then that we often see the world through a win/lose, two-alternative lens? Such a view is, of course, disastrous for the delicate process of achieving intimacy with another human being.

Control is a popular illusion closely related to the pursuit of perfection. In our dreams we could bend the world and the people in it to our will. Gone would be the need to negotiate differences, to endure the uncertainty of failure and rejection. Though we come to understand that such a world is impossible, sometimes we go to great lengths to achieve whatever control we can over those around us through the exercise of power or manipulation.

We all know people who are perfectionistic. They tend to be demanding of themselves and those around them and to manifest an obsessive orderliness that is, in the end, alienating. They do not trust feelings and prefer to occupy themselves with things they can count.

In defense of perfectionism, it might be said that obsessive people make the world function for the rest of us. Who, after all, wants to be operated on by a relaxed surgeon, or fly on an airplane maintained by mechanics satisfied when their work is "good enough?" If we excel at anything, it is because we are prepared to sweat the details (wherein resides either God or the devil, depending on your orientation).

The problem with perfectionists and their preoccupation with control is that the qualities that make them effective in their work can render them insufferable in their personal lives. I treat a lot of engineers and accountants and computer programmers. To be less controlling in their jobs would render them ineffective. The best one can hope for is to introduce them to the *paradox of perfection*: in some settings, notably in our intimate relationships, we gain control only by relinquishing it.

Life's two most important questions are "Why?" and "Why not?" The trick is knowing which one to ask.

Acquiring some understanding of why we do things is often a prerequisite to change. This is especially true when talking about repetitive patterns of behavior that do not serve us well. This is what Socrates meant when he said, "The unexamined life is not worth living." That more of us do not take his advice is testimony to the hard work and potential embarrassment that self-examination implies.

The reasons for what we do, for how we live, are often

obscure. We imagine that our behavior is, for the most part, a matter of conscious choice. Freud's major contribution to psychology was his theory of the unconscious mind, functioning below the level of our awareness and influencing our behavior. For many people, the idea that much of what we do is the product of motives of which we may be unaware is frightening. It is especially disconcerting when one is asked to pay attention to dreams and slips of the tongue to understand thoughts and impulses that we would rather not confront. As when President Nixon, in a speech before Congress during Watergate, said, "It is time to get rid of our discredited president . . . I mean present welfare system." (Or as when Condoleezza Rice began a story, "As I was telling my husb—As I was telling President Bush . . . ")

Once we acknowledge that there exists below our consciousness a swamp of repressed desires, resentments, and motivations that affect our day-to-day behavior, we have made an important step toward self-understanding. Once again paradox reigns. If we deny the existence of such an inner life (as did Nixon, who was terrified of psychiatrists), we will be surprised when our determined efforts at control collapse. (Why did he choose to tape and preserve the incriminating conversations that destroyed his presidency?)

Ignoring the existence of our subconscious tends to have

troubling results. We notice first the consequences of such unawareness: destructive patterns of behavior in which we find ourselves surprised that we repeatedly make the same mistakes.

To take a cultural cliché, what of the woman who chooses a series of men who resemble her father, right down to their alcoholism and penchant for abuse? Or the man whose several jobs all end unhappily in some conflict with authority? To change such habitual and maladaptive patterns of behavior requires first some recognition of the pattern. People tend to resist this, preferring to invoke coincidence or simply focus on individual events in a way that places responsibility on others. So if our man with authority problems also gets a series of speeding tickets, it is often hard for him to connect this with his job difficulties.

If people are reluctant to answer "Why?" questions in their lives, they also tend to have trouble with "Why not?" The latter implies risk. Steeped in habit and fearful of change, most of us are to some degree risk-averse. Particularly in activities that may involve rejection, we tend to act as if our sense of ourselves is fragile and must be protected. One would think that these fears would improve with age and experience; the opposite is usually the case. One of the most common and important pursuits, the effort to find a partner in middle age, is, for most, a frightening undertaking, burdened with hesitation and avoidance.

The struggle against loneliness is routinely associated with depression. The popularity of Internet matchmaking sites is testimony to the need for companionship. Because this culture enshrines youth and beauty and devalues older people, it is hard to feel desirable and confident enough to resume dating and consider intimacy in our middle years. Even our vocabulary betrays us; "boyfriend" and "girlfriend" seem odd characterizations for people in their 40's and 50's.

When presented with new things, the operative question may be "Why not?" but people frequently defend themselves from disappointment by asking "Why?" This can lead to the creation of endless excuses for not taking the chance implied in declaring oneself available. Many choose continued loneliness over the difficult task of getting to know new people, with its attendant risk of rejection. "All the good men are married" or "All these women have so much baggage" are refrains that I am accustomed to hearing.

I frequently ask people who are risk-averse, "What is the biggest chance you have ever taken?" People begin to realize what "safe" lives they have chosen to lead. The ways that people test themselves—contact sports, backpacking through Europe, military service—are foreign to most. Something is lost in our obsessive concern with safety and security—some spirit of adventure. Life is a gamble in which we don't get to deal the cards, but are nevertheless obligated to play them to the best of our ability.

The wager with the highest stakes of all is with our hearts. Where do we learn to do this? How do we balance the risk of making mistakes against the certainty of aloneness if we play it safe? Nowhere in our lives are the extremes of cynicism on the one hand and foolhardiness on the other so dangerous. Unlike most games, the outcome of this one is meant to reward everyone concerned. If we play as if this is a competition, we will lose. And yet, how do we determine that the other person shares a cooperative vision?

Here is where we must accept risk, sometimes a lot of it, in order to win. In no other activity do we expect to be skilled from the outset. Everyone accepts the idea of a learning curve accompanied by sometimes-painful mistakes before we become adept. No one would expect to become good at skiing without falling down. And yet many people are surprised at the hurt that routinely accompanies our efforts to find someone worthy of our love.

To take the risks necessary to achieve this goal is an act of courage. To refuse to take them, to protect our hearts against all loss, is an act of despair.

*Our greatest strengths are our
greatest weaknesses.*

There are certain personality characteristics that are highly correlated with academic and professional success: dedication to work, attention to detail, ability to manage time, conscientiousness. People who have this constellation of traits are generally excellent students and productive workers. They can also be difficult to live with.

Think about it; those who demand much of themselves frequently have high standards of performance for those around them. In a work situation, this is usually an adaptive approach. In one's personal life, the keeping of lists, perfectionistic attitudes, devotion to effort over pleasure and friendships, lack of flexibility, and stubbornness do not wear as well and tend to alienate those who value closeness, relaxation, and tolerance.

A certain amount of compartmentalization is necessary to succeed in the different areas of our lives. Juggling our multiple responsibilities—worker, partner, parent, friend—is a challenge. We think of ourselves as the same person whatever we may be doing at the moment. But our different roles demand different attitudes. If we try to impose a businesslike, vertically integrated decision-making structure on our families, we are likely to encounter resentment and resistance. Conversely, if our style tends to be impulsive, superficial, and pleasure-seeking, we may find it difficult to succeed at work.

One theme that is played out in many marriages is the coming together of someone with strong obsessive characteristics (usually a man) with someone else who has a more impulsive and theatrical personality (usually a woman). These people are initially drawn to each other because of complementary needs. The man is in need of more entertainment in his life and he values the woman as less inhibited, more spontaneous than he. The woman sees the well-organized and meticulous man as promising a measure of restraint that will balance her impulsive tendencies. It's easy to see why such a relationship often contains the seeds of disappointment and frustration. (He: "Why can't you be more responsible?" She: "You just don't know how to have fun.")

People with compulsive character structures are vulnerable to depression, as is anyone who seeks perfection in an imperfect world. It is often puzzling to such people that approaches that make them successful in their work are so poorly received by those they live with. Obsessive people put a strong emphasis on control. Anything that threatens this sense of being in charge induces anxiety. This leads inevitably to efforts to reassert control, in effect redoubling the behaviors that produced the problem in the first place. The resultant conflict produces feelings of frustration and discouragement that further reinforce a sense of failure.

Again, the "How's that working?" question can keep therapy within useful parameters, so that people are being challenged on a practical rather than a theoretical level. We all tend to get defensive if our deeply held convictions are challenged. This is why most political or religious arguments are fruitless. If we can be induced, however, to consider what we are doing on a purely pragmatic basis, we can sometimes be persuaded to try new approaches.

Practically any human characteristic—competitiveness, orderliness, even kindness—when indulged to an extreme can produce undesirable results. Perhaps this is just another argument for moderation in all things. But we need to acknowledge that those qualities of which we are most proud can prove our undoing.

We are face to face here with the sometimes confusing role of paradox in our lives. An example is the well-known advice to "be careful what you wish for." The longing and loves of our youth, so ardently pursued, often lead us toward some combination of amusement and regret in our later lives. Where is that girl we so desired in high school? Even if we are married to her, the person we fell in love with is a memory, as are, all too often, the feelings she inspired. The things we are sure will make us happy seldom do. Fate, it seems, has a sense of humor.

The list of paradoxes is endless: the relentless pursuit of pleasure brings pain; the greatest risk is not taking any. My personal favorite is the truth that *everything in life is a good news/bad news story*. The long-sought promotion brings more money and more headaches; our dream vacation puts us in debt; experience has taught us well, but now we are too old to use the knowledge; youth is wasted on the young.

Impermanence mocks us. Our efforts—to learn, to

acquire, to hold on to what we have—all eventually come to naught. This is the final and controlling paradox: *Only by embracing our mortality can we be happy in the time we have.* The intensity of our connections to those we love is a function of our knowledge that everything and everyone is evanescent. Our ability to experience any pleasure requires either a healthy denial or courageous acceptance of the weight of time and the prospect of ultimate defeat.

The most secure prisons are those we construct for ourselves.

When we think about loss of freedom, we seldom focus on the ways in which we voluntarily impose constraints upon our lives. Everything we are afraid to try, all our unfulfilled dreams, constitute a limitation on what we are and could become. Usually it is fear and its close cousin, anxiety, that keep us from doing those things that would make us happy. So much of our lives consists of broken promises to ourselves. The things we long to do—educate ourselves, become successful in our work, fall in love—are goals shared by all. Nor are the means to achieve these things obscure. And yet we often do not do what is necessary to become the people we want to be.

It is human to shift blame for our failures. Our parents come in for their share. We often cite lack of opportunity, as if life were a lottery with a limited number of winning tickets. A shortage of time and the requirement to make a living are common excuses for inaction. Also, the fear that we might try and not succeed can produce a crippling inertia. *Keeping our expectations low protects us from disappointment.*

We do not like to think of ourselves as trapped. This is, after all, the land of opportunity. We are surrounded by images of success. Our culture presents us constantly with stories of people who rose from obscurity to fame, often with limited talent. Rather than take hope from these stories, most people absorb them as additional indications of their own inadequacy. We are also confused and put off by the apparent ease with which these transformations occur. The slowness with which productive change actually takes place does not play well in an impatient society. Where do we find the determination and patience required to achieve the things we want?

There is no shortage of advice. Bookstores and magazines are full of suggestions about how to be wealthier, thinner, more assertive, less anxious, more appealing to the opposite sex. One would think that we are engaged in an orgy of self-improvement. And yet, the people I talk to, those brave enough to identify themselves as needing help, are, for the most part, doing pretty much the same things today that they did yesterday—and last year. My job is to point this out and wonder with them what it would take to make real changes in their behavior.

Before we can do anything, we must be able to imagine it. This sounds easy, but I find that many people do not make the link between behavior and feelings. I blame modern medicine and the advertising industry for much of this problem. We have become used to the idea that much of what we don't like about ourselves and our lives can be quickly overcome with little effort on our part. The marketing of medications that favorably affect our mood, changing our appearance through plastic surgery, and self-improvement through consumption all play into the fantasy that happiness is for sale. Malcolm Forbes famously suggested that, "Anyone who thinks that money can't buy happiness is shopping in the wrong places."

In fact, of course, such a belief only adds to our frustrations and renders our self-constructed prisons more secure. I think of this as a "lottery mentality." There are those who justify gambling by invoking the notion of selling hope. Those people standing in line, spending money they cannot spare in a game they have no plausible shot at winning talk endlessly about how they will spend their millions. This is not "hope" in any realistic sense; it is dreaming. I tend to confront patients who talk about changing their lives, but do not take concrete steps to do so. I often ask them whether their latest plan to do something different is a real expression of intent or simply a wish. The latter can be entertaining and distracting, but should not be confused with reality.

Religious transformation aside, alteration of our attitudes and behavior is a slow process; change is incremental. Look at any successful prison break and you will see plenty of imagination, hours of planning, often months, even years, of slow progress toward freedom. We may not admire the people who do this, but their ingenuity and determination are lessons for us all.

One of the most difficult things to ascertain when confronted with a person seeking therapy is their readiness to change, their willingness to exercise the fortitude that is necessary to do so. Some people seek help for reasons other than actually changing their lives. We live in a society that has elevated complaint to a primary form of public discourse. The airwaves and courts are full of victims of this and that: childhood abuse, mistakes of others, random misfortune. Voluntary behaviors have been reclassified as illness so that sufferers can be pitied and, where possible, compensated. Not surprisingly, many of these people appear in psychiatrists' offices expecting a sympathetic ear and medication that will relieve their feelings of distress. Often they want testimony to support lawsuits or letters to excuse them from work. They are not there to engage in the difficult process of examining their lives, taking responsibility for their feelings, deciding what they need to do to be happy—and doing it.

To clarify the role I am prepared to play I ask patients on first meeting to sign a letter that reads in part: *I do not get involved in work grievances, lawsuits, custody disputes, disability determinations, or other legal or administrative proceedings, including work excuses and requests for change in job conditions. If you require a medical advocate for any of the above reasons, you need to hire one elsewhere; I am here to provide therapy.*

People mistake thoughts, wishes, and intentions for actual change. This confusion between words and actions clouds the therapeutic process. Confession may indeed be good for the soul, but unless it is accompanied by altered behavior, it remains only words in the air. We are a verbal species, fond of conveying our minutest thoughts. (Remember the last time you listened to someone talking into a cell phone?) We attach excessive importance to promises.

Whenever, as happens frequently, I point out to people the discrepancy between what they say they want and what they actually do, the response is surprise and sometimes outrage that I will not take their expressions of intent at face value but prefer to focus on the only communication that can be trusted: behavior.

Probably the single most confusing thing that people tell each other is "I love you." We long to hear this powerful and reassuring message. Taken alone, however, unsupported by consistently loving behavior, this is frequently a lie—or, more charitably, a promise unlikely to be fulfilled.

The disconnect between what we say and what we do is not merely a measure of hypocrisy, since we usually believe our statements of good intent. We simply pay too much attention to words—ours and others'—and not enough to the actions that really define us. The walls of our self-constructed prisons are made up in equal parts of our fear of risk and our dream that the world and the people in it will conform to our fondest wishes. It is hard to let go of a comforting illusion, but harder still to construct a happy life out of perceptions and beliefs that do not correspond to the world around us.

The problems of the elderly are frequently serious but seldom interesting.

Old age is commonly seen as a time of entitlement. After long years of working, the retiree is presumably entitled to leisure, social security, and senior discounts. Yet all of these prerogatives are poor compensation for the devalued status of the elderly. The old are stigmatized as infirm in mind and body. Apart from their continuing role as consumers, the idea that old people have anything useful to contribute to society is seldom entertained.

The effort to isolate the old in their own institutions and communities bespeaks a belief that they have little to teach the rest of us and reflects a desire to decrease our interactions with them. That the elderly, like many minorities, cooperate in this segregation testifies to the power of stigma. Their ability to drive—that is, to retain their independence—is the subject of much humor and occasional official concern. (Did you know that in Florida cars are now being sold with a device that ensures that if a directional signal is left on more than twenty seconds, the car automatically turns?) Our fight against the physical signs of advancing age fuels a \$150-billion-a-year cosmetics industry that dwarfs in size other national priorities such as education, highway maintenance, or national defense. The rise of plastic surgery, potentially disfiguring injections of botulinum toxin, and a national preoccupation with wrinkles and hair loss all suggest that the normal process of aging evokes in most people a level of fear bordering on panic.

What we fear is our own demise, and indications of aging are simply unwanted reminders of our mortality. By rejecting old people and the signs of age in ourselves we are simply reacting to a natural fear of extinction that has preoccupied human beings forever. This is the cosmic joke. Fate or God or whoever is running this show appears to have said, "I will give you dominion over all other forms of life. BUT you will be the only species able to contemplate your death."

And what is the response of old people to being marginalized and devalued by society? They are angry. It's not enough that they must sustain the losses that come with age: diminished sexual attractiveness and enthusiasm, declining health, the death of longtime friends, a gradual loss of mental acuity. They must also deal daily with the disdain that society reserves for those without power or gainful employment.

And so it becomes the task of the elderly to complain. In our complex world certain groups are assigned certain roles. It is the job of teenagers, for example, to tax the rest of us with fast driving, loud behavior, and overuse of the word "awesome." Our senior citizens sometimes appear to exist in order to annoy everyone else with their slowness and physical complaints.

It is part of the symmetry of life that as we age we descend slowly back into infancy. This reassumption of a self-absorbed and dependent status in preparation for death is discouraging for all concerned. How, and how rapidly, this occurs defines what we have learned in our years upon this earth. One reason for our fear of aging is that those who have gone before us have, in general, set a poor example. Most families I talk to see their aging relatives as a burden. The idea that the elderly have anything to give the young in the way of wisdom and life experience is seldom considered. The reason: *most old people are preoccupied with self-centered complaints.*

When middle-aged people talk about their elderly parents, it is often with a sense of obligation mixed with discouragement. The old become more vulnerable to depression. Depressed people tend to be self-absorbed, irritable, and unpleasant to be around. Adequate treatment for depression is frequently denied the elderly. Pseudo-explanations substitute for medical evaluation: "I'd be depressed, too, if I were that old."

These lowered expectations on both sides result in a kind of standoff in which the elderly play their role as a source of endless grumbling while the young listen grudgingly and try to fulfill their obligations to their parents and grandparents with as little actual contact with them as possible. Segregation in separate living situations and the much-feared nursing-home commitment are two common indicators of the exclusion and marginalization that are frequent accompaniments of old age.

In fact, the stratification of society along age lines is one of its most rigid divisions, often exceeding separations created by education, wealth, and social class. When the elderly are still reasonably active, there occurs a kind of voluntary migration to warmer climates to gather in "retirement communities."

Florida and the Southwest are the most common destinations. The old frequently choose to live in places that exclude those below a certain age, usually fifty.

The effect of this self-segregation is to allow "seniors" to participate in the mindless pastimes that we associate with growing old: bingo, shuffleboard, golf, and "exercise classes" that appear to consist in movements so slow as to defy their purpose. What is virtually absent is contact with the young, except for obligatory family visits, as well as any hint of the intellectual stimulation that has been shown to sometimes delay the onset of dementia.

Incalculable harm is done to the relationship between the generations by the complaining (often accompanied by implications of neglect) that comprises the conversation of many of the elderly. I know lots of people who have come to dread phone calls from their parents and especially their answer to the question, "How are you doing?" What could be less interesting and more discouraging than a litany of aches, pains, and bowel difficulties, delivered in the querulous tone of those who realize that what they are suffering from is beyond remedy and getting worse?

I believe that parenthood, a voluntary commitment, does not incur a reciprocal obligation in the young—either to conform their lives to our parental preferences, or to listen endlessly to our protests about the ravages of time. In fact, I am of the opinion that the old have a duty to suffer the losses of age with as much grace and determination as they can muster and to avoid inflicting their discomforts on those who love them.

It is a primary task of parents throughout their lives to convey to the young a sense of optimism. Whatever other obligations we have to our children, a conviction that we can achieve happiness amid the losses and uncertainties that life contains is the greatest gift that can pass from one generation to the next. Like all the values we wish to teach our children—honesty, commitment, empathy, respect, hard work—the supreme importance of hope is taught by example.

Many old people report the feeling of invisibility experienced by other minorities. This takes the form of being ignored in stores by salespeople, seeing few desirable reflections of themselves in popular culture, becoming the object of obligatory visits and phone calls from family members, and above all, no longer being treated as if they have anything useful to say. It is this latter experience, not being listened to, that is the most galling for the elderly. The excruciatingly boring conversation that the old traditionally inflict upon the young is a kind of retaliation for the devaluation and sense of irrelevance that many old people feel.

"Getting old is not for sissies" is an accurate statement of the predicament faced by the old in a youth-obsessed society. Perhaps our final obligation is to sustain the physical and psychological blows that accompany our aging with a dignity that eschews self-pity.

Is it possible to remain hopeful in the face of the insults to our selfhood that time inflicts? Just as courage is a virtue not equally distributed among the young, so we cannot expect it to be uniformly demonstrated by the old. We know and value it when we see it, however. It is our ability to contemplate our imminent mortality with equanimity that gives us the opportunity, finally, to be brave.

If we can retain our good humor and interest in others even as the curtain closes, we will have contributed something of inestimable value to those who survive us. We will have thereby fulfilled our final obligation to them and expressed our gratitude for the gift of life that we, undeserving, have been given and that we have enjoyed for so long.

Happiness is the ultimate risk.

D epressed people tend naturally to focus on their "symptoms": sadness, loss of energy, sleep disturbance, appetite changes, diminished capacity for pleasure. It is easy to get caught up with trying, through medication and psychotherapy, to relieve these painful concerns. Sometimes, however, especially when my efforts to improve things seem ineffective, I redirect people's attention to the possibility that there might be advantages to their being depressed.

One of the benefits is that it is a *safe* position. The same, of course, could be said of chronic pessimism, which is often both a precursor and manifestation of depression. It is hard to disillusion pessimists; they are already discouraged and therefore immune to unhappy surprise. Because their expectations are chronically low, pessimists (who invariably see themselves as realists) are seldom disappointed. When I suggest to them that our expectations, good or bad, are usually met, they are skeptical since it has been so long since they have anticipated anything but the worst.

Asking someone to relinquish depression is often met with resistance. To be happy is to take the risk of losing that happiness. All significant accomplishments require taking risks: the risk of failure in invention, in exploration, or in love. We live in a society that is risk-averse. Enormous time and energy is devoted to promoting "safety" in all we do. We are taught to buckle our seat belts, lock our doors, refrain from smoking, get an annual physical, and consult our doctors before exercise. We worry about the weather, obsess about our children's security, live in houses with alarm systems, and arm ourselves against intruders.

The risks that previous generations took for granted: childhood mortality, infectious disease, environmental catastrophe, are not things that now preoccupy most people.

Instead, we have designated certain members of society—
police, firefighters, soldiers, athletes—to assume the risks
that the rest of us are afraid to take. Vivid depictions of
heroism in our entertainment are a source of much vicarious
excitement and provide distorted examples of what it means
to be brave. The links between violence, control, and courage
in these portrayals are inescapable and have little relevance in
our own lives.

It is often hard to sell unhappy people on the idea of
taking the chances necessary to alter attitudes and behaviors that play a role in their chronic discouragement. My
profession, psychiatry, has made some contribution to this
problem by its designation of depression as a chemical illness and its over-reliance on pharmacological solutions. In
this we have been abetted (and coerced) by insurance com-
panies, which have steadily eroded reimbursement for psychotherapy.

And what is psychotherapy? It is goal-directed conversation in the service of change. That's what people who come for
help want: *change*. Usually they want to alter the way they're
feeling: anxious, sad, disoriented, angry, empty, adrift. Our
feelings depend mainly on our interpretation of what is happening to us and around us—our attitudes. It is not so much
what occurs, but how we define events and respond that

determines how we feel. The thing that characterizes those who struggle emotionally is that they have lost, or believe they have lost, their ability to choose those behaviors that will make them happy.

Think about a person so disabled by worry that he can no longer function comfortably in the world. Every decision must be measured against the probability that it will increase or decrease anxiety. To the degree that one's choices become constrained by a need for anxiety avoidance, one's life shrinks. As this happens, the anxiety is reinforced and soon the sufferer becomes fearful, not of anything external, but of anxiety itself. People become afraid to drive, to shop, sometimes even to leave their houses. At this point some patients feel their choices in life have become so constricted that they withdraw from human contact. This same withdrawal can be seen in severe depression.

It is the job of the psychotherapist to re-instill hope. I frequently ask patients, "What are you looking forward to?" People who are overwhelmed by anxiety or depression often have no answer. The truly hopeless, of course, think about ending their lives.

When confronted with a suicidal person I seldom try to talk them out of it. Instead I ask them to examine what it is that has so far dissuaded them from killing themselves. Usually this involves finding out what the connections are that tether that person to life in the face of nearly unbearable psychic pain. There is simply no denying the anger embedded in any decision to kill oneself. Suicide is a kind of curse forever on those who love us. It is, to be sure, the ultimate statement of hopelessness, but it is also a declaration to those closest to us that their caring for us and our caring for them was insufficient to the task of living through another day. People in despair are, naturally, intensely self-absorbed. Suicide is the ultimate expression of this preoccupation with self. Instead of just expressing the sympathy and fear that suicidal people evoke in those around them, therapists included, I think it is reasonable to confront them with the selfishness and anger implied in any act of self-destruction.

Does this approach work to prevent someone from killing himself? Sometimes. In thirty-three years of practicing psychiatry I have lost this argument only once. A young mother of two, going through depression triggered by a bitter divorce, shot herself on the day she was to enter the hospital. When she didn't appear I met the police at her house and found her body. Whatever fantasies I had entertained about being able to control the life of another despairing human being left me that day.

And then, many years later, I received a phone call

telling me that my precious son, Andrew, age twenty-two, had ended his three-year struggle with bipolar illness by killing himself. Even now, thirteen years later, words cannot contain the grief that has been my companion since that awful day. It is an offense to the natural order of life for parents to bury their children. In a just world it would never happen; in this world it does.

When Andrew surrendered his long fight with despair, he left behind so many people who loved him and whose memories encompass an intermingling of the joy he brought us and the eternal sadness of his death. When I inventoried the record of his life that he left with me, I came across a school essay that he had written when he was nine. It reads in part:

> *It was about 2:30 PM and my father and I had been run-*
> *ning for over an hour. We were now heading into the*
> *wind so I got behind my father and he broke the wind*
> *for me. We were competing against 200 other runners.*
> *It was a hard course with many steep hills. In the last*
> *mile we increased the pace and passed several runners.*
> *When we reached the track, we had to go half way*
> *around it, and then we finished the thirteen-mile race.*

He was a wonderful student, president of his high school class, and had been elected to the student council as a sophomore at college when he was gripped by the first symptoms of his illness. He endured three hospitalizations and his moods oscillated wildly between manic disorganization and grinding depression. I imagine that his final desperate moments were eased with some anticipation of release from the anguish he had endured. I pray that he found at last the peace that he sought. Only this hope has allowed me to bear my own pain and go on.

His illness proved a cold wind that none of us could shield him from, and in the end it swept him away. He chose the too-soon moment of leaving, but I know he loved us as we loved him, and I have forgiven him my broken heart, believing that he forgave me all mistakes as his father. When I remember his laugh I hear the lyrics of an old Tom Paxton song:

> *Are you going away with no word of farewell?*
> *Will there be not a trace left behind?*
> *I could've loved you better,*
> *Didn't mean to be unkind.*
> *You know that was the last thing on my mind.*

14

True love is the apple of Eden.

I t is in the biblical story of the fall from grace and expulsion from the garden that Adam and Eve defined forever the traits that make us human: curiosity, weakness, and a desire for each other that transcends even our loyalty to God. What was it about that fruit that was irresistible, what made it worth trading a state of perfect, naked, and immortal bliss for a life of shame and toil? ("In the sweat of your face you shall eat bread.")

In some ways, the normal course of human development represents a prolonged version of the story of the fall. Childhood is a series of disillusionments in which we progress from innocent belief to a harsher reality. One by one we leave behind our conceptions of Santa Claus, the tooth fairy, the perfection of our parents, and our own immortality. As we relinquish the comfort and certainty of these childish ideas, they are replaced with a sense that, thanks to Adam and Eve, life is a struggle, full of pain and loss, ending badly.

When you think about it, it's remarkable that, instead of being hopelessly discouraged by such a state of affairs, we persist in trying to extract happiness from our brief time on earth. And of all the ways we pursue it, it is, as Genesis suggests, by "cleaving" to each other that we come the closest. (What an amazing word is "cleave," conveying at once opposite meanings: to split asunder and to hold fast.)

Mark Twain, in "Eve's Diary," put these words in her mouth after the fall: "When I look back, the Garden is a dream to me. It was beautiful, surpassingly beautiful, enchantingly beautiful; and now it is lost, and I shall not see it any more. The Garden is lost, but I have found *him*, and am content."

No one can, as I have, daily contemplate the detritus left behind by lost love without becoming a little cynical about the ways people choose those to whom they link their lives. Was this person completely different, I ask, at the moment you decided that you wanted to spend your life with him, came to believe that he should be the father of your children? Was there no hint of doubt about his loyalty, steadfastness, his love for you? The discussions that follow this question reveal, over and over, the shallowness and stupidity of our younger selves.

Perhaps it is the paucity of good examples with which we grow up. Few people I talk to admire what their parents demonstrated to each other in the way of affection and commitment. In fact, I frequently hear a kind of cynicism about the possibility of lasting love, based on what people have observed in the generation before.

It seems ironic that when people fall in love, no justification for their attachment is necessary. It is accepted that the process by which we are drawn to another is mysterious and beyond explanation. People talk about physical attraction, shared interests, some mysterious "chemistry" that pulls them together and makes them decide to share their lives. The people around them accept this and go ahead with the elaborate and expensive ceremony that will celebrate the beginning of their lives together. When, on the other hand, people fall *out* of love, the demands for an explanation are insistent: What happened? Who's at fault? Why couldn't you work it out? "We didn't love each other anymore" is not, in most cases, a sufficient response.

To a large extent this is an educational problem. One would think that such an important area of human behavior would be the subject of some consideration in the schools. Simon and Garfunkel, in their song "Kodachrome," summed up their secondary education as follows: *When I think of all the crap I learned in high school, it's a wonder I can think at all.* In the midst of such marginally relevant courses as trigonometry, industrial arts, and the ever-popular "health," one searches in vain for a course in human personality and behavior that contains useful information on how to avoid catastrophic mistakes in one's choice of friends and lovers. So, like most of life, the important task of choosing whom to fall in love with becomes another example of trial and error learning. If only the trials weren't so costly.

I could envision a curriculum constructed around the general topic "The pursuit of happiness." Instruction would begin with a discussion of the definition of love. Next would come some guidance on the subject of personality disorders, which would cover the characteristics of those most likely to break one's heart. There would follow a section called "Attributes of a successful marriage partner." Kindness and empathy and how to recognize the presence of these virtues would be discussed.

Finally, we would invite as guest lecturers people going through bitter divorces as well as those in successful long-term relationships. The latter would have to be chosen carefully. When I listen to comments from elderly people who have been married fifty, sixty, or more years answering the inevitable question about "the secret to a successful marriage," it seems to me that a high tolerance for boredom often heads the list. Such bromides as "We never went to bed angry" or "Moderation in all things" convey a philosophy more geared to survival than to pleasure. Where, one wonders, is the idea of endless, renewable love?

If Adam and Eve have anything to teach us with their spectacular fall from grace it is that the union of two people offers us the primary compensation for all the burdens of being human: the need to toil, the "thorns and thistles," and the lifelong knowledge of our mortality. What did that forbidden fruit contain that made its taste worth the anger of God? "*The Garden is lost, but I have found **him** and am content.*"

Only bad things happen quickly.

One of the common fantasies entertained by those seeking change in their lives is that it can be rapidly achieved. Once we "know" what to do it appears that we ought to be able simply to do it. That these sudden transformations are rare is a source of puzzlement to many.

The most familiar behaviors that are resistant to change are those that involve addictions of some sort: drinking, smoking, drug dependency. Here we postulate some chemical process at work that complicates our efforts to do what we know is best for us. The presence of withdrawal symptoms as we try to relinquish the unwanted substance confirms our belief that we are in the grip of a physical craving that overcomes our willpower and requires special programs to help us defeat it.

How about other apparent addictions like overeating and gambling (sex and shopping have recently been added)? Here the dependency is less obviously chemical, but anyone who has tried to control food intake or the desire to place a bet will tell you how difficult this can be.

What is at work here is the psychological power of habit. The characteristics that render each of us unique are seldom the products of rational choice. Sometimes, of course, we *do* choose to develop healthy practices. Regular exercise can be a life-enhancing routine. Our bad habits, however, tend to insinuate themselves over time and become extremely resistant to change, even when they threaten to destroy our lives.

Among these life-altering maladaptive behaviors are our habitual ways of relating to others. The traits that we display toward other people are major determinants of how successful we are in forming and sustaining relationships. Most of these elements of our personal "style" are not the products of conscious choice and are either inborn or were formed by our early experience with our families. Because they exist below the level of our conscious minds, they are resistant to change, even when they are evidently not working for us.

It is obvious that any process directed at changing, even a little, our well-established patterns of thinking and behaving is going to be an extended one and will involve efforts at gaining insight, reevaluating behaviors, and trying new approaches. Under the best of circumstances, such change takes time.

The same is true for all the other personal characteristics and habitual patterns that don't work for us but that we keep repeating: impulsivity, hedonism, narcissism, irritability, and the need to control those around us. To imagine that such traits can be changed overnight or as soon as we become aware of them is to discount the well-established strength of habit and the slowness with which we translate new knowledge into behavior.

When we think about the things that alter our lives in a moment, nearly all of them are bad: phone calls in the night, accidents, loss of jobs or loved ones, conversations with doctors bearing awful news. In fact, apart from a last-second touchdown, unexpected inheritance, winning the lottery, or a visitation from God, it is hard to imagine sudden good news. Virtually all the happiness-producing processes in our lives take time, usually a long time: learning new things, changing old behaviors, building satisfying relationships, raising children. This is why patience and determination are among life's primary virtues.

In a society based on consumption, the concept of instant gratification is pervasive. Advertising presents us constantly with images that suggest that happiness can be ours through ownership of material goods. Attractive people with lots of friends are shown enjoying themselves in a way that suggests that we might join them if we buy the correct car, the right house, the proper beer. One effect of these ads is to produce dissatisfaction with what we have and how we look. Another is to suggest the availability of a rapid antidote to our discontent: spending money. Is it any wonder that almost all of us are in debt?

The other things that are heavily advertised are nostrums of various sorts to cure problems that are uniquely modern. Any regular television viewer, for example, would think that we are in the midst of an epidemic of depression, allergies, arthritis, and gastroesophageal reflux disease. Every sneeze, every ache and pain is promised an easy cure through the taking of a pill.

Perhaps it was the invention of the automobile or the airplane or the telephone. Somewhere along the line we became an impatient people, expecting quick answers to all difficulties. Our penchant for technological solutions, so apparently successful in controlling our physical world, has had some unfortunate consequences when applied elsewhere. To cite an example for those of us who remember the 1960s, while John Kennedy lit the fuse on the rockets that would carry us to the moon, he also began to involve us in the most spectacular and expensive American failure of heart, mind, and technology in the twentieth century: the war in Vietnam.

Still we are encouraged to believe we live in a world where proper diet, exercise, and the judicious use of Botox and plastic surgery can dramatically slow the aging process. This modern pursuit of the fountain of youth bespeaks a lack of acceptance of our common fate. There is a desperate, superficial quality in trying to eliminate the gradual evidence of our mortality. (Someone has observed that, with the advent of healthy lifestyles, soon hospitals will be filled with old people dying of nothing.)

One of the things that make us human is the ability to contemplate the future. If we are to bear the awful weight of time with grace or acceptance, we have to come to terms with the losses that life inevitably imposes upon us. Primary among these is the loss of our younger selves. If we feel gradually devalued by becoming older, then our lives become a discouraging process marked by desperate attempts to look and act younger while we disregard the compensations of knowledge and perspective that should result from our accumulated experience.

Our attention spans are notoriously short. Events move past us with great rapidity. Our memories are consequently limited and we focus on the foreground. We pay attention to a limited number of mostly young, good-looking, and wealthy persons who fill the pages of one of our aptly named magazines: *People*. If they are the people, who are the rest of us? What does it signify to be obscure in a world preoccupied with fame, however earned or unearned? As long as we measure others and ourselves by what we have and how we look, life is inevitably a discouraging experience, characterized by greed, envy, and a desire to be someone else.

The process of building has always been slower and more complicated than that of destruction. Once I was a soldier. What turned me away from the profession of arms was *not* that I didn't enjoy blowing things up. In fact, I was afraid I enjoyed it too much. What I came to realize and to be offended by is that killing is such a simple-minded undertaking compared with preserving life. Our common future will be determined by the struggle between the killers and the peacemakers. One can always find justifications, frequently religious, for killing. As with anything else in life, however, it is the act that defines us, not the cause we use as a rationale.

This tension between simplicity and effort works itself out in our daily lives. If we believe in the sudden transformation, the big score, we are less likely to pursue the harder and less immediately satisfying work of becoming the people we wish to be.

So here's to the role of time, patience, and reflection in our lives. If we believe it is better to build than destroy, better to live and let live, better to be than to be seen, then we might have a chance, slowly, to find a satisfying way through life, this flicker of consciousness between two great silences.

Not all who wander are lost.

Americans are a linear people. We value discernible goals and see the straightest paths to them. Our educational system launches us on our stepwise journeys. The rules we are to follow are clear and involve obedience to authority, hard work, and cooperation with others. Original thought is prized within the confines of the hierarchical structures within which we are educated. We are taught to do what we are told until sufficient time elapses that we are allowed to tell others what to do.

Of all the things that define us, education appears to be the most highly correlated with success. It is little wonder, then, that we are urged throughout childhood to do well in school and take our successive graduations as necessary steps toward a comfortable life. There is a promise implicit in this process: follow instructions, please others, obey the rules, and happiness will be yours.

I talk to a lot of people, particularly men, who, in middle age, feel that the bargain they struck with the system has not been kept. Frequently, they are in secure jobs, own their own homes, have the requisite wife and 2.2 children, and feel lost. Much of what they aspired to now seems like a burden. They are preoccupied with what they might have missed.

Among the things frequently neglected in a linear, goal-directed life is sex. In a culture that is obsessed with it, practically no one feels that they have gotten their share. This is especially significant for men who are socialized to compete for attractive women and whose sense of themselves is closely tied to feelings of sexual adequacy. How else to account for the traditional identity crises that have men of a certain age pursuing affairs and buying sports cars? Often they tell stories of inhibited adolescences, early marriages, unsatisfying work, and a longing for excitement.

There was a time in the 1960s and 1970s when youthful

rebellion took the form of "dropping out." Disillusioned by what they saw as a world created by their parents' pursuit of materialism and alienated by the misbegotten war in Vietnam, many of the young simply refused to pursue the traditional paths to success. This "counterculture" was both feared and hated by the older generation, who focused on music they could not understand, drug use they condemned, and casual sex that they deplored and envied simultaneously.

The fact that most of these rebellious young people grew up to be white-collar professionals much like their parents does not detract from what they learned and taught the rest of us with their pleasurable detours. Long before, Stephen Vincent Benét put it this way: "For money is sullen and wisdom is sly, but youth is the pollen that blows through the sky, and does not ask why."

Even now there is a core of adventurous young people who are willing to step off the educational train long enough to see something of the world, join the military or Peace Corps, or otherwise educate themselves in ways not available in any classroom. Later in life, career changes, marital misadventures, spiritual explorations—all can be forms of "wandering" that seem to depart from the norm but may simply express the courage to take risks in the struggle to find happiness and meaning.

Back in the 1960s these quests were sometimes called "trying to find ourselves." (One cynical parent suggested that in the course of an especially prolonged search his child had time to find several people.) Though a straight line appears to be the shortest distance between two points, life has a way of confounding geometry. Often it is the dalliances and the detours that define us. There are no maps to guide our most important searches; we must rely on hope, chance, intuition, and a willingness to be surprised.

17

Unrequited love is painful but not romantic.

A t its heart, unrequited love is a longing for what we cannot have. Who among us has not felt its sting? Childhood and adolescent crushes that are not reciprocated give way to adult searches for the perfect partner. What we are looking for is someone we imagine will complete us and affirm our worth, and whose love will warm us in our old age. It is a powerful fantasy, seldom realized.

We seek the unconditional approval of the good parent, the ultimate in emotional security. If we got this as a child we want it again; if, like most of us, we did not, still we wish for it as a shield in an uncertain, often uncaring, world. Our desire to be accepted just as we are is so strong that we sometimes project our need for love onto another and ignore the fact that it is not being returned.

In their saddest form these feelings are directed at people we don't even know. Movie stars are frequent objects of adoration based on how they appear or the characters they play. Their privacy is routinely invaded by fanatical admirers convinced that they might somehow induce reciprocal feelings if only they were given the chance. Sometimes these frustrated emotions are transmuted into something different. John Hinckley's fantasies about Jodie Foster gave us all a lesson in the power of unrequited love.

The line between romantic love and obsession is frequently blurred. The key difference is that an obsession can reside in one person alone. It is a close cousin to delusion, a false belief that is a cardinal symptom of a disturbed mind. What differentiates love, requited or not, is that it is a form of admiration, unlike, for example, a conviction that one is being followed or persecuted by the government. The latter is an unappealing and self-centered belief, while pining after someone has a dreamy, idealistic quality that appeals to our need to hope against hope.

One step up from the dangerous obsessions of the stalker is the love that will not die. This quality is frequently on display in battered women and those for whom a dead relationship is still the subject of endless contemplation—and conversation. I have heard a lot of stories that begin, "He hurt me, he left me, but I still love him." It is as if proclaiming one's undying devotion dignifies what could otherwise be mistaken for an unattractive masochism.

"Love at first sight," another popular, though mindless, fantasy, sets us up for disappointment. The sudden wave of feeling and the appeal to a powerful, almost spiritual, event short-circuits the task of building a friendship that can deepen into something more electrifying. The latter takes time, attentiveness, and some level of rational thought. We may also experience an emotion less easy to comprehend and explain than shared interests and sexual attraction, but this does not mean that "falling in love," though dizzying, is akin to stepping off a cliff in the dark.

What gives love its power is that it is *shared*. When experienced alone, the feeling we are having may be intense, as is any form of loneliness, but it is not likely to persist or result in any useful behavior and is of limited interest to others.

There is a mythical organization for singles, "Sex Without Partners," that has a membership composed of many who suffer from unrequited love. Application is free and you can participate without leaving home.

There is nothing more pointless, or common,
than doing the same things and expecting
different results.

M istakes are a consequence of being human and constitute an essential element of trial and error learning.
Some errors are more consequential than others; few are irredeemable. What is frustrating is the experience of making the
same mistake repeatedly. This phenomenon is especially evident in the way that people choose others with whom to be
intimate. Someone has suggested that a second marriage represents the triumph of hope over experience. One might

intuitively expect that the lessons learned in the first marriage would make the selection process for the second more informed. Alas, the failure rate in subsequent marriages exceeds even the 50 percent that characterizes our first, youthful lunges into matrimony.

The reality behind these numbers is that we tend to be the same people, philosophically and behaviorally, at forty as we were at twenty. This doesn't mean we have learned nothing in the intervening years. In fact, most people complete their educations in this time and become more successful occupationally. We just haven't gained equivalent insight into who we are and why we choose the people we do.

The process of learning consists not so much in accumulating answers as in figuring out how to formulate the right questions. This is why psychotherapy takes the Q&A form that it does. This is not, as many think, a trick on the therapist's part to lead the client in a known direction. It represents a joint exploration, an inquiry into motives and patterns of thought and behavior, trying always to make connections between past influences and present conceptions of what it is we want and how best to get it.

Much, perhaps most, human behavior is driven by intentions that are below the level of our awareness. Since we like to think of ourselves as rational people doing things for explainable reasons, it is disconcerting to acknowledge that much of our habitual conduct is determined by needs, desires, and experiences of which we are only dimly aware and that are related to our past experience, often from our childhoods.

For example, the act of "forgetting" can often be understood as representing an unconscious commentary on the subject of our inattention. Why do dentists' offices routinely call patients to remind them of appointments? Because going to the dentist is for most of us an unpleasant experience. It is common, therefore, for people to "forget" their appointments. When we forget other things: birthdays, anniversaries, names, promises, it is also possible to discern underlying attitudes that may be hard for us to acknowledge openly.

So it is with our choice of people to be with. *Nearly every human action is in some way an expression of how we think about ourselves.* There are few behaviors that are "self-esteem neutral." I frequently suggest to patients that this criterion can be applied to any important life decision: How will this make me feel about myself? In particular, how does being with this person make me feel? Can we say with Jack Nicholson's character in *As Good as It Gets*, "You make me want to be a better man?"

Our repetitive mistakes are most noticeable in the family dramas that play out over and over again in a way that suggests long rehearsal. My most frequent question to someone who describes a familiar episode of marital conflict is, "How did you think this conversation would go if you said that?" If traced to its beginnings, one can almost always find in any dispute some direction, criticism, or outright insult that the other person reacted to with predictable antagonism. For example, a patient recently reported that his response to an early-morning complaint from his wife was, "Stop whining!" Predictably, their day went downhill after that. When wondering with someone why they felt it necessary to say something that leads to conflict, the answer often turns out to have a defensive or retaliatory tone: "Aren't I entitled to defend myself?"

It is surprising how often the closest relationships in our lives come, over time, to resemble power struggles in which we become intimate enemies. Gone is the sense of shared fate, replaced by a daily battle in which the stakes appear to be a survival of self-respect that is somehow threatened by the person who knows us best. Who would want to live this way, in a state of hyper-alertness and competition for stakes that are obscure, even for the participants?

And yet, when people are asked to stop making the disparaging comments that are at the root of much marital conflict, they shift responsibility for change from themselves to "the other" in a way reminiscent of international conflicts in which everyone wants peace, but no one wants to be the first to cease retaliation, fearing that it will just make them vulnerable.

At the heart of such skepticism is mistrust. And so, it seems, is the case with many relationships. My argument in such situations is usually some variation on, "What have you got to lose by trying?" The response is often, "How long do I try?" A better question might be, "Why would I live with someone I don't trust?" But this is seldom asked, since it brings up all the reasons that people coexist for years in unhappy relationships: money, concerns for children, fear of being alone, and simple inertia.

The sad fact is that most people have a low expectation of happiness. It is as if they have relegated the whole idea to the realm of myth that, like Santa Claus or the tooth fairy, has been discredited by their life experience. They regard any lasting sense of joy as a romantic ideal propounded by the entertainment industry, of no more relevance to their own lives than million-dollar houses or private jets. This disillusionment is a major barrier to change, since people cannot be expected to take emotional risks in pursuit of goals they think impossible.

Encouraging people to change is an exercise in shared hope. Most of us, no matter how cynical we may be about improvement in our own lives, wish for something better for our children. Often I invoke this desire to get people to try new things. The leverage here is the common belief that children learn the majority of what they know about life from observing their parents. I regularly use this idea to try to persuade people to try to set examples of kindness, tolerance, and conflict resolution on their children's behalf.

Here is where the concept of repetitive behaviors leading to predictable results comes in. Most people are sufficiently attuned to the experimental method and the concept of cause and effect to appreciate that, if what they have done in the past has produced unsatisfying outcomes, a new approach may be worth considering. I frame this argument in pragmatic rather than theoretical terms: "I don't have answers applicable to every relationship; I believe in what works. What you are doing now isn't working. Why not try something else?"

We flee from the truth in vain.

A t age thirty-four I was undergoing psychoanalysis as a part of my residency training. One day my analyst informed me that I was adopted. I was, at the time, lying on a couch and had been "free-associating" about a conference I had been to recently at which a group of adult adoptees had talked about searching for their birth parents. My analyst asked me what I would do in their place and I responded that I would certainly search. He then said, "Start looking."

"What are you saying? I'm adopted?"

"Yep."

"How the hell do you know?"

He knew because, in a breathtaking breach of therapist/client privilege, my estranged wife's psychologist had approached my analyst at a party and asked, "Does Dr. Livingston know he's adopted?"

My analyst replied, "He hasn't mentioned it."

It turned out that my wife had heard the news years before through family friends, but thought it was my parents' choice to tell me or not. She discussed it with them and they declined. So she told her therapist, her therapist told mine, and he had to figure out a way to bring it into the one-sided conversation that is psychoanalysis. I will always be grateful that he had the courage to do so.

At the time, I found the information disconcerting. My parents had never mentioned the subject. I had wondered at times why my father, an avid photographer, had never taken any pictures of me before the age of one. I also wondered how it happened that I had been born in Memphis when they were then living in Chicago. My father worked for the government and he explained to me that they had been in Tennessee on temporary assignment. My official birth certificate, which clearly indicated that I had been born to them, was, of course, a lie.

My mother died shortly before I found out about my adoptive status. The conversation with my father was difficult. I alternated between anger at the deception and understanding for his fear that, if I knew, I would somehow be less *his* son. Truth to tell, I was excited about finding out who I was biologically connected to, and a little relieved that I was not genetically destined to be just like him. I felt free, curious—and a little weightless. My father could remember few details of the adoption and swore he had never known my real name. This statement also turned out to be false.

I traveled to Memphis and engaged a lawyer who, through local knowledge and sleight of hand, obtained the record of my adoption, which had been sealed by the court those many years ago. There was the name I was born to, David Alfred Faulk, and my birth mother's name, Ruth. It turned out that I had been left in the clutches of the Tennessee Children's Home, a notorious baby-selling operation abetted by a corrupt judge who provided court-ordered relinquishments. The agency had placed children with well-to-do parents all over the country. I called my father and asked him how much he had paid for me. Many people wonder what they're worth. I know: $500.

The lawyer told me to leave the searching up to him. "You don't know what you'll find. Some of these babies were born to patients from the state mental hospital." I figured I could handle whatever or whomever I discovered. I was also certain that knowing was better than not knowing.

The first people I found were members of the foster family that had kept me for the first year of my life. I had only a last name when I began calls to people in the Memphis telephone directory. On about the tenth call I made I explained who I was and I heard the man at the other end turn to someone and say, "Hey Ma, it's Bo." The matriarch was a lady in her eighties who, when I visited, brought out a studio-taken baby picture of me at about six months of age. Her husband had run a gas station. None of her children had gone to college. I tried to imagine myself now with a Tennessee drawl and a mechanic's uniform with "Bo" on the patch. The whole family gathered to welcome me back. They said my birth mother, who had left me with them, was from Vicksburg, Mississippi.

I started calling people named Faulk in the Vicksburg phone book and soon was talking to my mother's sister. This time I said that I was the son of a friend and asked where Ruth was. Her sister said she lived in Atlanta and worked for a book publisher. I traveled there and called her. I told her who I was and that I'd like to meet her. When the apartment door opened I saw someone who looked a lot like me. She asked, "What took you so long?"

She had been a schoolteacher from a religious family, pregnant out of wedlock by a man who wouldn't marry her but offered to finance an illegal abortion. She declined, traveled to Memphis, gave birth, and left me there, intending, she said, to come back. When she finally called the agency, it was too late. She never married, "didn't feel entitled." She taught elementary school and eventually changed grades each year to correspond to the grade she knew I would be in. She never forgave herself for "not living up to the moment." She was relieved that things had turned out well for me. I thanked her for my life.

I was, of course, curious about my birth father. Ruth gave me his name. He had died a few years before, leaving behind a daughter. I found out where she was and called her, thinking that I, an only child, at last had a half-sister. She was glad to hear from me, but it happened that she too was adopted. She was thinking of searching for *her* birth parents.

So, are we related, we two children of the same father? What must he have thought, unable to conceive a child with his wife while carrying the secret of a son cast adrift? His daughter sent me a picture. It is all I have of him. I know how the children of dead soldiers must feel, looking at old photographs of fathers they cannot remember or never met. I imagine that I see sadness in his eyes. If only I could speak with him for a moment, to tell him that things turned out all right, that something good came from his passionate mistake. If I cannot love him, I wish I could give him peace.

20

It's a poor idea to lie to oneself.

Authenticity is a prized ideal. Though required to play a variety of roles in our daily lives, we would like to see ourselves as having a relatively stable identity that expresses our core values over time. Most of us also place a lot of importance on the way we are seen by those whose opinions we respect.

There are few human attributes that excite more contempt than hypocrisy. People whose actions do not accord with their professed beliefs become objects of derision. Most of the scandals that entertain us are based on a disconnect between words and behavior: adulterous preachers, deceitful politicians, drug-abusing moralists, pedophile priests. Our outrage is balanced by our fascination, fueled by the guilty knowledge of our own failure to conform our behavior to the standards we publicly endorse. What would people think if they knew?

Worse than the concealment of embarrassing moral lapses are the interpretations that allow us to continue doing things that erode our sense of ourselves. We routinely invoke theories of accident, coincidence, and forgetfulness to explain behaviors that we do not wish to examine closely. For example, discoveries of infidelity are now routinely made by one spouse discovering incriminating e-mails left by the other on the family computer. (This is a variation on the more traditional diary-left-out-where-it-could-be-read method.)

Denial is another way people lie to themselves. Those indulging addictions commonly assert that they do not have a problem and can quit at any time, assertions that fly in the face of a catastrophic decline in their lives: DWIs, broken marriages, lost jobs. I often tell such people that it's understandable that they might feel a need to lie to others, but lying to ourselves disables us entirely from making needed changes.

I know a man who has repeatedly struck his wife at night

while in the grip of an agitated dream that he cannot quite remember. Because this is "accidental," it is never the subject of much reflection about the nature of the relationship. Less dramatically, millions of couples sleep in separate rooms because of loud snoring by one or the other. Surely, no blame could attach to such a (literally) unconscious behavior.

The most damaging lies that we tell ourselves involve promises. "Nothing is so beautiful as a promise, right after it is given." The evanescent quality of New Year's resolutions constitutes a cultural cliché. Good intentions are more than paving stones on the road to hell, they are distractions from the serious task of evaluating who we are and what we really want. If we spend our time imagining some ideal of beauty or self-improvement, it drains energy and distracts our attention from more serious and attainable objectives.

While no one can deny the role of chance in human affairs, it is an act of laziness to ascribe to luck most of what happens to us. Once again, people are reluctant to take responsibility for themselves, preferring easy excuses to difficult self-examination. This is another form of self-deception that leads nowhere. Of course accidents occur. If someone is struck by lightning in an open field it is hard to blame him; if he is struck while standing under the only tree in sight, then one might question his knowledge of celestial electricity.

We are daily confronted with examples of "death by stupidity." Drunk driving, diseases related to smoking or obesity, accidental discharge of firearms—all take their toll and remind us of our vulnerability to our own worst impulses. What do people tell themselves about these risks? If we hazard our lives for another or for an ideal we are acting bravely. But as Sancho Panza observed to Don Quixote, "to die without good reason is the greatest sin."

The truth may not make us free, but to lie to ourselves in the name of temporary comfort is the ultimate folly. Such deception appears to be a benign dishonesty. No one else is cheated or disadvantaged, but life decisions not based on reality are bound to be faulty. To see ourselves plainly is, perhaps, impossible; it's hard to get through the day without a rationalization or two. It is when our dream of what we could be collides with the truth of what we are that the clang of cognitive dissonance both deafens and blinds us.

We are all prone to the myth of the perfect stranger.

N
o element of dissatisfaction with our lives is more common than a belief that we have in our youth made the wrong choice of partner. The fantasies generated thereby often take the form of a conviction that there exists somewhere the person who will save us with his or her love. Much of the infidelity that is the hallmark of unhappy marriages rests on this illusion.

Some estimates of marital infidelity by age forty place it

at fifty to sixty-five percent of married men and thirty-five to forty-five percent of married women. In a society whose dominant expressed marital value is monogamy, these are numbers that indicate not just a high level of hypocrisy, but some serious dissatisfaction with our partners. What is it that people are looking for outside their marriages?

What is sought, apart from variety, is reassurance. In some respects every pleasure-seeking activity is a response to our fear of death. As we age and try to come to terms with the futility of our desires for youth and immortality, one response is to seek out experiences that feed our conceit that we retain our attractiveness. What better way to do this than through sex with someone new?

A healthy process of maturation allows us to internalize a belief that we are uniquely valuable, and gives us a stable sense of a lovable self. But this is an ideal outcome; more often people look with varying degrees of desperation for someone to love them unconditionally and are troubled that this is asking too much. That we seldom get this approval from our spouses is a source of gnawing but unmentioned discontent in most marriages.

In fact, what passes for love between adults more often resembles a kind of unspoken contract for services. Traditionally, this took the form of an implicit agreement that the man was responsible for financial security while the woman provided housekeeping, sex, and child care. The women's movement resulted in a renegotiation of the contract to include the desire of many women to work outside the home and a reluctance to take sole responsibility for child rearing and household chores. These laudable steps in the direction of gender equality had as one side-effect a heightened sense of resentment and competition in many marriages.

It became an article of faith for feminists that no one relinquishes power willingly; it has to be seized. This attitude is not a prescription for increased closeness. When combined with an increase in the financial independence of women, it is perhaps not coincidental that one in two marriages now ends in divorce. In some ways this change appears to be a good thing. People are less likely to be trapped in unsatisfactory relationships. Any social development that increases our choices seems like an improvement, so why do we live with a sense that we have lost something important?

First, there is the damage that is being inflicted on children. The comforting reassurance that it is better for them to adapt to parental separation than live in unhappy marriages has come to seem more like a rationalization for adults in pursuit of their own happiness. There is ample evidence that the dissolution of marriages results in tremendous insecurity and unhappiness for children, particularly since most of the time there is some level of bitterness and recrimination between their parents. That kids are able to cope in some way with their lives being turned upside down does not alter the devastation and disillusionment that most of them experience.

Because of these consequences and financial considerations, most infidelity is not undertaken in anticipation of divorce, though divorce is often the result. It represents at one level a kind of promiscuity that is evident among nearly all animal species. In another respect, infidelity is a uniquely human expression of fear and longing. The search for ideal love is both infantile and a symptom of middle-aged fears. That it most often fails to improve our lives, indeed frequently devastates them, does not dissuade us from trying.

Long ago Joan Baez sang, "You go running off in search of the perfect stranger . . . " The name of the song was "Fountain of Sorrow."

22

Love is never lost, not even in death.

I am a parent twice bereaved. In one thirteen-month period I lost my oldest son to suicide and my youngest to leukemia. Grief has taught me many things about the fragility of life and the finality of death. To lose that which means the most to us is a lesson in helplessness and humility and survival. After being stripped of any illusions of control I might have harbored I had to decide what questions were still worth asking. I quickly realized that the most obvious ones—Why my sons? Why me?—were as pointless as they were inevitable. Any appeal to fairness was absurd.

I was led by my fellow sufferers, those I loved and those who had also endured irredeemable losses, to find reasons to go on. Like all who mourn I learned an abiding hatred for the word "closure," with its comforting implications that grief is a time-limited process from which we all recover. The idea that I could reach a point when I would no longer miss my children was obscene to me and I dismissed it. I had to accept the reality that I would never be the same person, that some part of my heart, perhaps the best part, had been cut out and buried with my sons. What was left? Now *there* was a question worth contemplating.

Gregory Peck, in an interview many years after his son's death, said, "I don't think of him every day; I think of him every hour of every day." With time the nature of these thoughts changes, from the lacerating images of illness and dying to softer memories of all that their lives contained.

Grief is a subject I have come to know well. Indeed it was *the* subject of my life for a long time. I wrote a book about it, trying to find my way around it. What I learned is that there is no way around it; you just have to go through it. In that journey I experienced hopelessness, contemplated suicide, and learned that I was not alone. Certain that there could be no comfort in words, I came to realize that words, my own and those of others, were all I had to frame my experience, first my despair and finally a fragile belief that my life still had meaning.

Thirteen years later, my sons, though frozen in time, remain a living presence for me. I have, largely, forgiven myself for not being able to save them. I have reconciled myself to growing old without them. They will not, as I once confidently assumed, bury me. I have forsaken any belief in an orderly universe and a just God. But I have not relinquished my love for them nor my longing that, against all reason, I will see them again.

This is what passes for hope: those we have lost evoked in us feelings of love that we didn't know we were capable of. These permanent changes are their legacies, their gifts to us. It is our task to transfer that love to those who still need us. In this way we remain faithful to their memories.

At my daughter's wedding I borrowed some thoughts from Mark Helprin and constructed the following toast:

The love between parents and children depends heavily on forgiveness. It is our imperfections that mark us as human and our willingness to tolerate them in our families and ourselves redeems the suffering to which all love makes us vulnerable. In happy moments such as this we celebrate the miracle of two people who found each other and created new lives together. If love can indeed overcome death, it is only through the exercise of memory and devotion. Memory and devotion . . . with it your heart, though broken, will be full and you will stay in the fight to the very last.

23

Nobody likes to be told what to do.

It seems too obvious to mention, and yet look how much that passes for intimate communication involves admonitions and instructions. I sometimes ask parents of balky children to keep track of the percentage of their interactions that consists of criticism or directions (the latter being a variation on the former). I'm used to hearing numbers like eighty to ninety percent. Sometimes, not surprisingly, communications between the parents themselves yield similar figures.

How are we inclined to react when told what to do? For most of us, resentment progressing to obstinacy is the most common response. Whether our refusal is overt ("Not going to do it") or passive-aggressive ("I forgot"), the result is commonly frustration all around. We are not obedient people. Most of us are the descendants of those who undertook dangerous voyages in pursuit of freedom and self-determination, and were willing to sacrifice a great deal in defense of these ideas. We are genetically programmed to question authority.

Still we try to tell each other what to do. Our desire for control and a belief that we know how things *should* be overcomes our common sense about how people react to orders. This is especially true of parents. Even in our child-centered (some might say child-obsessed) society, we think we know best how to "guide" our children so that they will fulfill their above-average potential as students, athletes, and American success stories.

Often I ask people in conflict to *withhold criticism* of those around them to see if this changes the atmosphere. It is amazing how radical this suggestion seems to many people. The thought seems to be, "If I give up criticizing and directing those around me, chaos will ensue. Chores will not be done, dishes will pile up, rooms will not be cleaned, the house will fall down, homework will be ignored, school failure will ensue, followed by drug abuse, pregnancy, and a life of crime. I can't let that happen!" This is called "awfulizing," the idea that any relaxation in standards or vigilance is the first step toward failure, degradation, and the collapse of civilization as we know it.

This essentially pessimistic view of human nature underlies much of what passes for child-rearing lore. The "terrible twos," for example, are supposedly the time when the intense self-centeredness of infancy collides with the parental need to say "no." The resulting temper tantrums are felt to be an early rehearsal for the inevitable adolescent struggles over autonomy. There is a kind of self-fulfillment in the way that parents shake their heads knowingly as they discuss these developmental stages with each other. As with most things in life, our expectations are generally realized.

Another way to view the conflicts that arise between parents and children is that they are skirmishes in a long-term power struggle based on the faulty assumption that the primary task of parenthood is to shape the behavior of children through incessant instruction enhanced by the application of rules and punishments. While this approach sometimes works, more often it produces oppositional children who grow into oppositional adults.

Passive resistance is the last refuge of the powerless.

Assembly line workers who cannot strike *can* slow down. Children, who are prevented by their small physical and psychological size from confronting their parents openly, can demonstrate their unhappiness by not doing what they are told. Poor schoolwork, failure to do assigned chores, extreme slowness, a tendency to ignore instructions—all are common examples of passive-aggressive behaviors that drive parents crazy. The most common parental response is to persist with lectures, instructions, and punishments in an effort to "get this kid to listen."

I often ask people if they really think that lack of understanding on the child's part is the problem. Do they believe that one more lecture will prove persuasive? Or does the problem reside in the coercive, repetitive, and critical nature of the relationship?

Not infrequently, those who are preoccupied with issues of control with their children have similar difficulties in their interactions with their spouses. The marital climate is typically characterized by bickering, power struggles, and a sense on both sides that they are not being heard. Once again I ask people to imagine a situation in which criticism and instructions are withheld. People used to giving their spouses lists of assigned tasks find it hard to imagine alternatives ("He forgets everything!").

Since judgmental people were generally raised in judgmental families, they find it hard to envision another way of interacting with those they live with. To ask them to do so is to expect them to change habits of long standing. Conscious effort and a modicum of good will are necessary. The latter is often hard to come by in relationships that have long been characterized by disapproval and defensive hostility. It is always easier to keep doing what we're used to, even if it's evidently not working for us.

The idea that it is possible to live without criticizing and directing everyone around us is a novel one for many people. If someone can be persuaded not to do this, even for short periods, the result is customarily one of relief. The belief in discipline is akin to the Catholic concept of Original Sin that holds we are all born with a stain on our souls that we must expiate—with the help of our parents and the church. We must be saved from our basest impulses. The primary incentive for submitting to these authorities is fear: "*The wages of sin is death.*" This is why the most fundamentalist faiths have the strictest child-rearing practices. What is at stake is not just one's earthly success or failure, but one's immortal soul.

Whether we are religious or not, all of us are caught up to one degree or another in the fantasy that children are blank slates upon which parents inscribe the rules. It is our job to teach them everything they need to succeed in the face of internal impulses and external influences that threaten to ruin them. Many parents are afraid that they are not up to the task, that they will fail and their children will be lost. Too often, in our efforts to be good teachers, all we transmit is our anxiety, uncertainty, and fear of failure.

The primary goal of parenting, beyond keeping our children safe and loved, is to convey to them a sense that it is possible to be happy in an uncertain world, to give them hope. We do this, of course, by example more than by anything we say to them. If we can demonstrate in our own lives qualities of commitment, determination, and optimism, then we have done our job and can use our books of child-rearing advice for doorstops or fireplace fuel. What we cannot do is expect that children who are constantly criticized, bullied, and lectured will think well of themselves and their futures.

24

The major advantage of illness is that it provides relief from responsibility.

People enter my office in great distress. No one drops by to chat. The cost of psychotherapy and the stigma associated with any form of emotional disorder ensure that those who seek help are in pain. Many of them are surprised, therefore, when I ask them if their difficulties present any advantages. They are so used to focusing on their discomfort and the limitations imposed by their anxiety or depression that it has never occurred to them that there could be any sort of payoff associated with these conditions.

One of the basic rules of animal psychology is that any behavior that is reinforced will continue; behavior that is not will extinguish. A monkey will pull a lever for a long time if he is rewarded by food, even at intermittent and unpredictable intervals. If the food stops completely, the lever-pulling will, over time, cease. So it is with people. We do those things repetitively that produce some reward. It is just hard sometimes to discern what that reinforcement might be.

Of all the burdens that weigh on our lives, being responsible for ourselves and those we care for can be the most onerous. People endure numbing routines, jobs they hate, unsatisfying relationships, all in order to fulfill the expectations they have of themselves. When no other relief is available to us, some form of illness or disability is one of the few socially acceptable ways of relinquishing the weight of responsibility, if only for a little while.

Instead of being expected to get up each morning and face tasks that we abhor, we are, when sick, told to "take it easy." For some people, trapped on a treadmill of obligation, the disadvantages of diminished functioning and physical pain are counterbalanced by the relief of lowered expectations.

Most people, of course, do not think in these terms.

Preoccupied by the obvious *disadvantages* of their illness, they resent any implication of secondary gain. And yet, especially in cases in which people receive some form of relief from work or other responsibilities, it is hard to escape the possibility that this might play a part in reinforcing and prolonging the sick role.

It is also true that the longer someone is disabled, the greater the chance that the illness will become a part of a person's identity—the way we think of ourselves. This is a dangerous development in that those aspects of our characters that we incorporate into our sense of ourselves are subconscious and resistant to change. It is the therapist's job to bring these things to awareness where they can be understood and dealt with.

Psychiatric diagnoses are necessarily descriptive. We have no idea what causes people to be vulnerable to extreme anxiety. Since the condition runs in families and responds to medication, it is fair to postulate that it has some inherited, biological basis. Genetic research will no doubt eventually clarify the specific, chemically mediated mechanisms involved, but will we then know why siblings, even identical twins, differ in the degree to which they experience this condition?

It has been a failing of traditional medicine that it has promoted in most people a sense of helplessness in the face of physical illness. This has increased the dependency on and the status of doctors at the expense of a sense of responsibility in patients. The rise of effective somatic treatments—antibiotics, surgery, drugs to control conditions like diabetes, hypertension, all manner of hormone deficiencies—has contributed to the sense that healing is something that happens to us rather than something in which we are active participants. This attitude has had the effect of inducing a kind of passivity in those afflicted by physical disease. By the same token, the discovery in the last fifty years of medications that are efficacious in the treatment of anxiety, depression, and psychotic illnesses has created the expectation on the part of those suffering from these conditions that taking a pill will be sufficient to relieve their suffering.

While medication has certainly earned a place in the treatment of a multitude of emotional disorders, the continuing importance of psychotherapy in helping people change their feelings and behavior remains undiminished. The translation of good intentions into behavioral change remains the province of the extended educational process that is therapy. The essential message of such an undertaking—that each person is responsible for the choices he or she makes in our never-ending quest for happiness—retains its power as an instrument of transformation.

We are afraid of the wrong things.

We live in a fear-promoting society. It is the business of advertisers to stoke our anxieties about what we have, what we look like, and whether we are sexually adequate. A dissatisfied consumer is more apt to buy. Likewise, the purveyors of television news attempt to hold our interest by scaring us with stories of violent crime, natural disasters, threatening weather, and environmental hazards ("Is your water safe to drink? Details at eleven.").

One of the things that define us is what we worry about. Life is full of uncertainty and random catastrophe. It is easy, therefore, to justify almost any anxiety. The list of fears that people carry with them is long and varied, and a function of the information with which we are bombarded.

People who are anxious to begin with are especially prone to specific fears. In their most exaggerated form these are called phobias. Imagine being afraid to go to the grocery store, ride an elevator, drive a car, cross a bridge. And don't even think about flying. Each of these represents a common phobia, an irrational but disabling fear. In a way, people who avoid such things are like sentinels for the rest of us whose fears are less obviously immobilizing, though they may be no more realistic. Reaction to the terrorist attacks of 2001 provides an illuminating example of how public fear can have profound consequences. People in large numbers sold their stocks and stopped flying. Airlines were pushed into bankruptcy. Then came the anthrax scare; the public became afraid of their mail and suppliers of gas masks sold out. The home of the brave looked like an asylum for anxiety sufferers.

When, in 2002, the Washington, D.C. area endured three weeks of random sniper attacks, there was a virtual panic, with people altering their lives and school systems canceling field trips and keeping children indoors. "If we can save one life the precautions are worth it," was a common refrain. No one pointed out that the logical extension of this philosophy would be to never leave home again.

Even in good times the public perception of the risk of becoming a crime victim is exaggerated. We arm ourselves against mythical intruders and ignore the reality that family members are the most likely victims of the guns we buy. Meanwhile, the real risks to our welfare—smoking, overeating, not fastening seat belts, social injustice, and the people we elect to office—provoke little anxiety.

Just as phobias serve as a distraction from more fundamental and troubling fears—loneliness, for example—perhaps the things that terrorize us as a group serve a similar function in the life of the nation. If we are focused on SARS, mad cow disease, killer bees, or prowlers in the night, we are less likely to pay attention to environmental degradation or the erosion of civil liberties, problems that may seem entirely beyond our individual ability to influence. Even war seems to have little effect on the anxiety of any except those with family members at risk.

Our relations with each other are characterized by mistrust. Instead of a sense of shared fate and the capitalistic idea that we can all prosper together, we often behave as if life is a competition that we can only win at the expense of others. We live with the fear of being sued. At some level I know that every patient I see is a potential adversary if there is a "bad outcome." For other medical specialties—obstetricians, surgeons, or emergency doctors—the likelihood and consequences of error are much higher and malpractice premiums are elevated to the point that some doctors are leaving medicine.

What would happen if we changed our legal system so that awards to people who were injured by the mistake of another were limited to economic damages? If it was felt necessary to punish corporations for outrageous negligence, that money could take the form of a fine that, instead of going to any individual or his attorneys, would become part of a "misfortune fund" that could be used to compensate people facing extraordinary expenses that were no one's fault (e.g., parents of children born with disabling abnormalities, victims of crime or natural disasters). Surely this would be fairer and more compassionate than enriching a few winners in the litigation lottery.

Such a system would reinforce the belief that we all share in the inevitable uncertainties and risks that are a part of life. It would certainly be a more equitable acknowledgment that, while we can be compensated for economic loss, no amount of money can (or should) make up for the random suffering that is our common fate.

We are bombarded by images of those who have succeeded with little or no effort or ability: trust fund babies, lottery winners, reality show participants, no-talent entertainers. This naturally leads to distortions in our sense of what is valuable or lasting. Our own lives and relationships seem pedestrian by contrast.

If our cultural icons are flawed, our political leadership is no more inspiring. The level of intelligence and integrity displayed by those we elect to office is generally unimpressive. In fact, it sometimes seems that our political system is designed to select those whose narcissism and hunger for power overwhelm their professed concerns for the welfare of their fellow citizens.

Rather than be afraid of these real threats to our well-being, we are easily persuaded that our maximum danger resides in some foreign place inhabited by those who wish us ill. We are all too easily manipulated by our fears into believing in military solutions to human problems. Like the carpenter whose only tool is a hammer, every problem looks to us like a nail.

Though unpleasant to experience, fear can be an adaptive emotion if it results in actions that protect us from harm. For this to happen, however, threats must be identified realistically. This requires accurate information and the ability to integrate it into useful knowledge. If we are deceived by those we trust to inform us (our government), or if our sources of information have a stake in keeping us afraid (the news media), then it is little wonder that we spend our time worrying about remote threats like contaminated mail, while ignoring real risks such as global warming.

And so it is in our personal lives as well. Fear and desire are opposite sides of the same coin. Much of what we do is driven by fear of failure. A primary example is the pursuit of material wealth. This is also the engine that drives our economy and a way of "keeping score." But this effort lacks ultimate meaning for most of us and distracts us from activities and people that provide more lasting pleasure and satisfaction. If it is true that no one on their deathbed wishes that they had spent more time in the office, what does that suggest for redirecting our efforts now?

Much of our behavior is driven by some combination of greed and competition. The successful entrepreneur is the model for the American success story. Donald Trump is a cultural icon. Success in business seems like a confirmation of the Darwinian concept of the survival of the fittest. The quality or usefulness of the work is insignificant compared to the wealth it generates.

Fear, while effective in the short term, is not useful in producing lasting change. The use of it as a motivator for behavior ignores the fact that there are no more powerful desires than the pursuit of happiness and the struggle for self-respect. If means can be found that move people in these directions: better jobs, education, the chance to improve one's life, and a sense of fairness and opportunity, the seductive and short-lived bliss provided by drugs will lose its appeal. Punitive emphasis on the "supply side" has not worked. Reducing the demand by emphasizing treatment and social alternatives to hopelessness offers the only prospect of winning this struggle between transient pleasure and lasting satisfaction.

The sum of our fears is the knowledge of our vulnerability to random misfortune and the certainty of our eventual mortality. If we can take comfort and meaning from some religious belief with its promise of eternal life, so much the better. But even skeptics can learn to savor the moments of pleasure that our brief lives contain. It is not denial but courage that allows us to do this. That and an unwillingness to let the present moment be drained of joy by fear of the future or regret for the past.

Parents have a limited ability to shape children's behavior, except for the worse.

At the college my daughter attended they devote a section of the graduation issue of the student newspaper to baby pictures of the graduates with brief comments from each set of parents. Almost all of these messages contain some variation of the following: "We're so proud of you." It seems a natural feeling at such a moment, but my sense is that embedded in that pride is a certain amount of public self-satisfaction in the evidently great job we have done as parents.

We appropriate to ourselves some of the success rightly earned by our children.

I was struck by this because I see in my work the other side of this coin: parents whose children are *not* doing well, who are on illegal drugs, in trouble with the law, or in some other way failing in their lives. These parents are beset with guilt ("What did we do wrong?"). Their child's struggles reflect poorly on their own efforts. You seldom see a bumper sticker that reads, MY KID IS IN REHAB.

To imagine that we are solely, or even primarily, responsible for the successes and failures of our children is a narcissistic myth. It is obvious that parents who abuse their children—physically, psychologically, or sexually—can inflict serious and lasting damage upon them. It does not follow, however, that parents who fulfill their primary obligation to love their children and provide a stable and nurturing environment for them to grow are responsible for the outcome of their kids' efforts.

As their own people, our children succeed or fail primarily because of the decisions, good and bad, that *they* make about how they will live their lives. Parents can try to teach the values and behaviors that they have found to be important, but it is the way we live as adults that conveys the real message to our children about what we believe in. Whether they choose to integrate these values into their own lives is up to them.

Kids have a keen nose for hypocrisy. The enduring popularity of *The Catcher in the Rye* among teenagers attests to this. If there are major contradictions between what we say and what we do, our children are likely to notice and be cynical, but as independent human beings, they bear the ultimate responsibility for how they incorporate into their own lives what they have seen or learned in childhood.

Anxiety is contagious. Children sense it in their parents and are affected by it. This begins at an age when the child has no words for the emotions she experiences and senses in the people around her. For most new parents the process of bringing a child into their lives is complicated and fraught with uncertainty. The physical demands, especially the change in sleep patterns, are difficult. To worry about whether they are "doing it right" is natural. The sources of information and support are of variable quality. One's own parents may or may not have anything useful to say, and the myriad books on parenting often contain conflicting advice (e.g., the enduring debate about "picking the baby up when she cries").

One of the major disagreements among experts applies to the subject of "discipline," and, like most of our core beliefs, has political overtones. The conservative method is based on the assumption that children are intrinsically self-centered and need to be "socialized" through the setting of firm limits accompanied by punishment for transgressions. The expectation is that child rearing is a series of power struggles that the parents must win and that it is perfectly legitimate to use one's greater psychological and physical size to ensure victory.

Much advice revolves around teaching politeness and tractability—and the ways in which parents can inhibit the natural tendency of children to disrupt the family in their heedless and irresponsible pursuit of pleasure. Such a view, of course, is an expression of the fundamentalist concept of mankind as sinful and restrained only by the strict imposition of proscriptive rules ("Thou shalt not . . .").

Alternatively (and there are many alternatives), parents can adopt a less rigid, more optimistic assumption, namely that, given love and support, most children grow into happy, productive adults independent of whatever theory of parenting they were raised with. This more relaxed approach tries to set reasonable limits on children's behavior, and is apt to provoke less confrontation and resentment. It is applied in the spirit of knowing that success in parenting is not dependent on a certainty that one is right or has all the answers. It is imperative not to hit kids since fear and violence are the primary lessons taught by corporal punishment.

The significant thing that I have observed over the years is that children can be raised successfully under a variety of parental regimes ranging from the authoritarian to the permissive. What is important is that children feel loved and respected. It is essential for parents to establish limits, especially around questions of safety and aggression. At the same time, most of the debilitating struggles within families that drain the happiness of all concerned and lead to destructive power struggles flow from an obsessive need for control on the parents' part and an anxious sense that their direction is all that stands between their children and a life of crime. When parents are preoccupied with unimportant issues like food consumption and room cleanliness, these will be arenas for endless conflict.

Anyone who has spent time in airports is aware of the disadvantages of parental overindulgence of unruly children. The question becomes how to foster a decent respect for the rights of others without engaging in meaningless exercises of authority that depend on fear and that ultimately induce resentment and passive-aggressive resistance.

As with so many things in life, danger exists at the extremes. What may appear to be an authoritarian/permissive spectrum is, in fact, more like a circle in which children raised in homes where parental control is severe turn out to have a poor set of internalized limits because they have experienced only rigid external rules. Conversely, in families where there are few constraints children do not have a way to learn those guidelines necessary to live comfortably with others.

Our primary task as parents, beyond attending to the day-to-day physical and emotional welfare of our children, is to convey to them a sense of the world as an imperfect place in which it is possible, nevertheless, to be happy. We can only accomplish this by example. What we say pales in comparison with what our children see us do.

So, when parents, convinced of their crucial roles in shaping the futures of their children, ask me, "What can I do to make sure this kid turns out well?" they are often surprised at my response: "Not much, but maybe cutting down on the fights and not trying to control your child's every decision might help to make everyone happier right now."

A vivid example of how parents inflict their worst fears on their children can be seen in the hysteria that surrounds the issue of stranger abductions. Though fewer than 200 children each year are taken by strangers in this country, the publicity surrounding the subject brings parents out in droves whenever there is a "child safety" program at the local mall. Usually this involves such things as fingerprinting and photographing children. If kids ask why this is being done, parents are hard-pressed to answer honestly: So that we can identify your body if you're kidnapped. Do we think that children cannot sense our fear? Meanwhile, 3,400 children die each year in motor vehicle accidents and 5,000 are killed by the accidental discharge of firearms.

It is infinitely discouraging to encounter a pessimistic young person. At an early age they have already decided that life holds little prospect of turning out well. Where did they learn this? Not, in general, from reading the newspaper.

When people wish to defend their cynical outlooks, they seldom lack for evidence. It is not hard when examining our lives or the world around us to find support for the belief that things are going to hell in a handbasket. Bad news is inherently more interesting than good and so we are daily inundated by stories of tragedy, chaos, and the depths of depravity to which human beings are capable of descending. It sometimes seems surprising that we're not *all* clinically depressed (instead of the fifteen to twenty percent of us who actually are).

How can anyone be happy in such a world? A good case of healthy denial helps, but the real secret is selective attention. If we choose to focus our awareness and energy on those things and people that bring us pleasure and satisfaction, we have a very good chance of being happy in a world full of unhappiness. It is the true wonder of the human condition and the ultimate demonstration of courage that we can bring ourselves, even momentarily, to enjoy life even as we are surrounded by evidence of its brevity and potential for disaster.

The ability to do this, to be happy with each other, constitutes the most useful example we can provide our children. A sense of humor helps, too.

The only real paradises are those
we have lost.

Nostalgia for an idealized past is common and usually harmless. Memory can, however, distort our attempts to come to terms with the present. When people speak wistfully of the way things used to be, it is almost always in contrast to what is happening now and reflects a kind of gloom about the future.

In our memories, things were less expensive, crime less common, people more friendly and trustworthy, relationships more enduring, families closer, children more respectful, music better. My parents lived through the Great Depression. They lost their savings in a bank closure, lived hand to mouth through the 1930s. Yet, in their later years, even this experience took on a romantic hue as they recalled neighbors helping neighbors survive the shared adversity and contrasted it with the selfishness that they saw all around them in the modern world of their old age.

Things were not really better long ago. War and genocide were as common then as now. Children regularly died of infectious diseases. Crime and poverty were widespread. Humans have not been, on balance, more virtuous for any extended period of history.

What happens as we try to come to terms with our pasts is that we see our lives as a process of continual disenchantment. We long for the security provided by the comforting illusions of our youth. We remember the breathless infatuation of first love; we regret the complications imposed by our mistakes, the compromises of our integrity, the roads not taken. The cumulative burdens of our imperfect lives are harder to bear as we weaken in body and spirit. Our yearning for the past is fueled by a selective memory of our younger selves.

Some years ago, I went to the funeral of a colleague. He

had been an admirable person, sensitive to others, and a good doctor. One of the people who spoke recalled his "wonderful sense of humor." I turned to a friend sitting next to me and asked, "Did John have a sense of humor?" If so, I had seen no evidence of it in the years I had known him, and I wondered if this desirable quality, like a medal for a dead soldier, could be awarded posthumously.

Whenever I go to the funeral of someone I have known well, I marvel at the image of that person that is portrayed in the eulogy. Seldom does their imperfect humanity survive the idealized descriptions that, while meant to comfort, succeed only in sanitizing the life of the deceased. To know someone fully and love them in spite of, even because of, their imperfections is an act that requires us to recognize and forgive, two very important indicators of emotional maturity. More important is the fact that, if we can do this for other people, we may be able do it for ourselves.

It is our fallibility and uncertainty that make us human. Our constant challenge is not to seek perfection in ourselves and others, but to find ways to be happy in an imperfect world. We are impeded in this effort if we cling to an idealized vision of the past that insures dissatisfaction with the present.

Memory is not, as many of us think, an accurate transcription of past experience. Rather it is a story we tell ourselves about the past, full of distortions, wishful thinking, and unful-filled dreams. Anyone who has been to a high school or college reunion can attest to the selectivity and variability of memory. How could people recall shared events so differently? The answer, of course, is that what we remember and how we remember it are affected by the meaning of events to us and by the effort we all make to construct a coherent narrative from our lives that reflects what we think of ourselves and how we became the people we are—or wish we were.

I often hear people marvel at the different ways they recall their upbringing when talking with siblings. Even people raised in the same house by the same parents are fre-quently left with distinctly different recollections of what happened to them. One will remember abuse, while another will deny it. Much frustration and resentment can result from these dissimilar memories, which often derive simply from the fact that people see themselves differently in the present, and as a result, they have different narratives of how they got here.

We are reluctant to revise our personal mythology. Dis-tant or abusive fathers, controlling mothers, marital strife and dissolution, all make their appearance here. We have absorbed the notion that our destinies are shaped by our childhood experiences. There is a poster showing a sparsely populated auditorium with a banner in the background that reads, "Adult Children of Normal Families."

Conversely, I also hear of idealized upbringings that sound like *Leave It to Beaver* reruns. In these versions of the past, parents were loving and attentive with hardly a cross word for each other or their children. My professional skepticism about these stories is often met with resentment, as if I were stealing something valuable.

Other intimate connections that turned out badly can also be cited as reasons for the caution or mistrust that affect our ability to risk our hearts again. Perhaps more destructive are memories of "the one that got away." It is common for people to have someone in their pasts whom they recall with longing and regret, someone to whom they adversely compare all subsequent relationships. This person can be a parent, a first love, or a friend no longer here. Their perfection, like that of a funeral eulogy, is a function of selective memory that can no longer be tested by daily contact. They exist in a sort of distracting dream with which the people now in our lives cannot compete.

The problem with our longing for the paradises of the past is that it distracts us from our efforts to extract pleasure and meaning from the present. Nostalgia also sends a message to those around us who did not share in our golden youth that the world they inhabit is inferior and getting worse. As our own powers decline and we are in increasing need of the kindness and attention of others, this seems to be the wrong message to give them.

The young frequently look at the old with a combination of obligation, disdain, and fear. They ask themselves, is this what I have to look forward to? Will I become a collection of physical complaints and recurrent reminiscences of an earlier, better time? It is hard enough to come to terms with our mortality without having to experience the depression that is such a routine accompaniment of old age. "The good news is that life expectancy is increasing; the bad news is that the extra years are tacked on at the end."

Who has not had the experience of meeting someone from the past with surprise as our memory is tested against present reality? This is not, as we are inclined to imagine, just a function of the way people change over time. When we visit our childhood homes, we are commonly amazed at how much smaller they seem. It is we, of course, who have grown larger.

When Russell Baker first submitted the memoir of his youth, *Growing Up*, it was rejected by a publisher as uninteresting. He then told his wife, "I am going upstairs to invent the story of my life." The result was a best seller—and no less true than the original version. Each of us has similar latitude in how we interpret our own histories. We have the power to idealize or denigrate those characters that inhabit our life stories. We just need to experience both alternatives as reflections of our current need to see ourselves in certain ways, and to realize that we are all able to color our pasts either happy or sad.

If we lack the ability to see the past clearly, we might concede that holding on to a romanticized version is just another way of sabotaging the present. When, in the maturity of our years, we sense that the likelihood of achieving earthly perfection or complete happiness is small, we have the choice of accepting and enjoying what we have made of our lives. Or, we can long for a simpler time, when all seemed possible and hope prevailed over our limited experience. It is this state of innocent optimism that we long to regain even as the limitations of time and chance weigh us down.

We are haunted by paths not taken, especially our missed opportunities for perfect love. As we age, our bodies betray us and our opinions can harden into calcified prejudice. And from this unenviable vantage point we look back on the Elysian fields of our youth when the possible outweighed the probable in our estimate of the future. It is this state we wish to regain and it is puzzling to us that our memories can be such a curse on the present.

So, how best to recover hope when the western horizon of our lives looms increasingly close? We can cultivate religion with its promise of immortality and reunion with those we have lost. Or, we can concede a poor agnosticism and surrender ourselves to the unknown as we try to imagine some meaning in the ceaseless rhythms of existence: life and death, dream and despair, and the heartbreaking mystery of unanswered prayers.

Of all the forms of courage, the ability to laugh is the most profoundly therapeutic.

With all due respect to the concept of ambivalence, people find it hard to entertain two emotions simultaneously. For example, one of the standard behavioral antidotes to anxiety is deep muscle relaxation. If one teaches anxious people to relax their skeletal muscles, they have a tool they can use when they find themselves in situations that habitually produce the sweating, rapid heartbeat, hyperventilation, and sense of doom that are the standard components of a panic attack.

It is revealing to ask those in the grip of depression when was the last time they laughed aloud. It is even more useful to ask family members to try to recall the last time they saw the patient amused. I am accustomed to hearing answers ranging from months to years.

So what? What is important about laughter in our lives? Some people treat humor as a minor distraction from the serious business of living rather than an important component, and indicator, of a happy life. If you ask people, even when they are depressed, if they have a good sense of humor, the answer is nearly uniformly "Yes." (People also universally identify themselves as good drivers, in spite of ample evidence to the contrary.) If someone appears to be especially dour while claiming a sense of humor, I sometimes ask him to tell me a joke. I know that this is, for many, an unfair request, since the ability to pay attention to and remember things that have amused us is highly variable. Many people are at a loss. So I tell *them* a joke, such as the current "world's funniest story" established by voting on a British Web site:

Two New Jersey hunters are walking through the woods. Suddenly, one of them collapses and is not breathing. The other whips out his cell phone and calls 911. "My friend is dead!" he tells the operator. She says, "Take it easy, I can help you. First you need to make sure he's dead." There is a silence and she hears a gunshot. The man comes back on the line. "OK. Now what?"

People's reactions vary. Many are so unaccustomed to finding anything funny that they have lost the capacity for surprise that is the essence of humor. Others, of course, are simply unprepared for the idea that a psychiatrist might try to amuse them. Sometimes I give those who appear terminally humorless the homework assignment of coming up with a funny story before our next meeting.

All this may seem trivial when confronting the weighty issues of despair and anxiety that bring people to therapy. But what gives humor its power in our lives is that a capacity for laughter is one of the two characteristics that separate us from other animals. The other, as far as we know, is the ability to contemplate our own death. There is a connection between these two uniquely human attributes that cuts to the heart of the great paradox of life: *It is possible to be happy in the face of our mortality.* What allows us to do this is not just what has been labeled "healthy denial." All humor is in some way directed at the human condition. To laugh at ourselves is to acknowledge the ultimate futility of our efforts to stave off the depredations of time. Like the New Jersey hunter, we are in the grip of forces we cannot control, including, often, our own stupidity; yet we do not give up.

To be able to experience fully the sadness and absurdity

that life so often presents and still find reasons to go on is an act of courage abetted by our ability to both love and laugh. Above all, to tolerate the uncertainty we must feel in the face of the large questions of existence requires that we cultivate an ability to experience moments of pleasure. In this sense all humor is "gallows humor," laughter in the face of death.

There is ample evidence that humor heals. Norman Cousins devoted a book to his own experience of curing himself from a debilitating, undiagnosed disease using little more than old Marx Brothers movies. It makes sense that the internal chemical changes brought about by laughter have a salubrious effect. They are a subcategory of the well-documented benefits derived from an optimistic, healing attitude. The mind/body interplay is at the heart of every theory of how we can influence recovery by the ways in which we think and feel about whatever afflicts us. Long before the advent of modern medicine, faith healers of various descriptions mobilized people's attitudes to combat disease. That this approach works is beyond question. People still travel to Lourdes and the piles of crutches and wheelchairs outside the grotto attest to the power of faith.

What you don't see there, of course, are artificial limbs. There are limits to the "miracles" being wrought. What does seem to be taking place is some form of accelerated healing based on the belief of the afflicted that God will make them well. The results are commonly miraculous enough.

Humor also is a form of sharing, an interpersonal exercise. To share laughter is a way of affirming that we are all in this lifeboat together. The sea surrounds us; rescue is uncertain; control is illusory. Still we sail on—together.

I saw a patient with his wife recently. "He never laughs anymore," she complained. The man agreed: "My sense of humor is gone." They had recently been on a trip and she had lost her wallet and credit cards. "The same thing happened to my wife," I said. "Her credit cards were stolen. But I haven't reported it yet because the thief is spending less than she does." The man laughed. My wife, when I told her the story, did not.

Pessimists, like hypochondriacs, are right in the long run. Nobody gets out of here alive. But pessimism, like any attitude, contains within it a multitude of self-fulfilling prophecies. If we approach others in a suspicious or hostile way, they are likely to respond accordingly, thereby confirming our low expectations. Fortunately, the opposite is likewise true. As with any rule there are exceptions and those we encounter do not always mirror our attitudes. If habitual optimism cannot protect us against occasional disappointment, habitual pessimism is a close cousin of despair.

We usually smile when we meet people for the first

time. When we do so we are conveying more than friendliness. Smiling is an indication of "good humor," and represents an acknowledgment of the joke embedded in our common humanity: *Things may be grave but they need not be serious.*

Mental health requires freedom of choice.

The salient characteristic of any form of emotional disorder is that the person who has it is constrained in some way. People suffering from depression, anxiety, bipolar illness, or schizophrenia are prevented from functioning freely in the world and have to adjust their behavior to compensate for their illness.

When we are depressed our loss of energy, inability to concentrate, and sad mood customarily cause us to withdraw from the people and activities that previously gave us pleasure. Our ability to work is compromised and in extreme cases we lose our will to live altogether. Similarly, excessive anxiety usually results in various avoidance behaviors that attempt to reduce the worry and nervousness with which we are beset. In the case of major mental illness, manic depression or schizophrenia, our loss of touch with reality prevents us from engaging the world freely.

All of the conditions I have mentioned have a biological basis, which is why medication is generally effective. To the degree that our functioning and relationships are affected, however, it is important also to take a behavioral approach to treatment. In the case of a life constricted by anxiety, people need to muster the determination to confront their fears and stop giving in to them. This approach manifests the cardinal rule of anxiety: *Avoidance makes it worse; confrontation gradually improves it.*

In the case of depression, the behavior that needs changing generally involves overcoming inertia and fatigue enough to do things that predictably make us feel better. This is a lot to ask when someone is discouraged, pessimistic, and feeling worthless.

Even people whose grasp of reality is shaky are usually not that way all the time. For them the struggle to change makes use of whatever benefit their medication provides to live as normal a life as possible. When one is dealing with chronic mental illness, strong and informed family support is essential. The most profound lessons about love I have learned in the course of my work have been taught by the parents, spouses, and children of those disabled by Alzheimer's or schizophrenia or developmental handicaps. Most medals for heroism are awarded for brief occasions in which people behave bravely. Those who, day in and day out, care for a disabled loved one are seldom recognized but have, in my mind, earned a special place in whatever heaven there may be.

I was at a conference recently where a presenter was reflecting on the burdens of chronic illness and he mentioned an organization for disabled people that he felt was especially helpful. As he paused, trying to remember the name of the group, the voice of a man in a wheelchair was heard throughout the large auditorium: "Not . . . Dead . . . Yet!" "Yes," the speaker responded, "that's it!"

There is a lesson for all of us in such determination. It's not simply that we're fortunate that there are people whose burdens are greater than our own. It is that every life contains losses. How we respond to them is what defines us. The Compassionate Friends is an organization of parents who have lost a child. Many such bereaved people report being told by well-wishers, "I don't know how you stand it; I'm not sure I could." This comment, meant as a compliment, provokes a kind of bitter amusement in grieving parents. What choice do we have? Are we to die ourselves and abandon those who still depend on us? In many ways our own death would be preferable to the prospect of life without the lost loved one, but that relief is denied us so we bear what we must and soldier on.

Mental health is a function of choice. The more choices we are able to exercise, the happier we are likely to be. Those who are most unwell or discouraged suffer from a sense that their choices have been limited, sometimes by external circumstances or illness, most often by the many ways we restrict ourselves. The primary variable in this regard is tolerance of risk. If we take counsel of our fears, particularly our fear of change, it is hard to choose a life that makes us happy. Is it anxiety or lack of imagination that restricts us?

We are never out of choices, no matter how desperate the circumstances. This, more than anything, is the stuff of psychotherapy, to empathize with the burdens that people bear without giving in to despair, conveying always the conviction that all is not lost. We are not dead yet.

Forgiveness is a form of letting go, but they
are not the same thing.

L ife can be seen as a series of relinquishments, rehearsals for the final act of letting go of our earthly selves. Why, then, is it so hard for people to surrender the past? Our memories, good and bad, are what give us a sense of continuity and link the many people we have been to the one that temporarily inhabits our changing body.

The collection of habits and conditioned responses that renders us unique serves as a kind of gyroscope, lending our responses to life a predictability that is of value both to us and to those who seek to know us. Our former selves can also serve as a sort of anchor, providing stability while sometimes inhibiting adaptation to new circumstances.

Few of us had ideal childhoods. It is easy to get caught up in self-definitions that involve past traumas as explanations for why our lives are not what we wish. The problem with living in the past is that it inhibits change and is therefore inherently pessimistic.

Certainly it is true that understanding who we are depends on paying attention to the history of our lives. This is why any useful psychotherapy includes telling this story. Somewhere between ignoring the past and wallowing in it there is a place where we can learn from what has happened to us, including the inevitable mistakes we have made, and integrate this knowledge into our plans for the future. Inevitably, this process requires some exercises in forgiveness—that is, giving up some grievance to which we are entitled.

Widely confused with forgetting or reconciliation, forgiveness is neither. It is not something we do for others; it is a gift to ourselves. It exists, as does all true healing, at the intersection of love and justice.

To acknowledge that we have been harmed by another but choose to let go of our resentment or wishes for retribution requires a high order of emotional and ethical maturity. It is a way of liberating ourselves from a sense of oppression and a hopeful statement of our capacity for change. If we can relinquish the preoccupations and pseudo-explanations that are rooted in the past, we are free to choose the attitudes with which we confront the present and future. This involves an exercise of consciousness and determination that is a certain antidote to the feelings of helplessness and anxiety that underlie most of our unhappiness.

As we contemplate the inevitable losses that we have had to integrate into our lives, the way we grieve and the meaning that we assign to our experience determine how we face the future. The challenge is to remain hopeful.

Many people choose a religious basis for their hope. The idea that we live under the guiding hand of a merciful God and are promised life everlasting is a great comfort that answers for many believers the universal question, and shortest poem, of human existence: "I, why?" Religion also provides a way of dealing with the uncertainty and apparent randomness of serious loss since it ascribes purpose to all human events and we are relieved of the burden of understanding by a simple acknowledgment that God's ways are both inscrutable and ultimately benign.

Those like me, unable or unwilling to relinquish our

skepticism about easy answers to large questions, are left with the difficult task of living with uncertainty. Not for us is the comfort of religious formulations. Instead we must struggle to establish some basis of meaning for our lives that does not depend on a belief in a system that requires continual worship of a deity that created us and gave us a set of instructions, which, if followed, will defeat the death that is our common fate.

Some form of forgiveness is the end point of grieving. My six-year-old son died from complications of a bone marrow transplant performed in an effort to cure his leukemia. I was the donor. Coming to terms with his death—not accepting, not closure, and certainly not forgetting—has been an exercise in forgiveness: for the doctors who recommended the procedure and for myself whose marrow failed him.

When I prayed for his life it was an act of desperation fueled by the hope that the religion of my youth might yet save what was most precious to me. When he died, a victim of random cell mutation within his otherwise perfect body, I was left with the conviction that no god who would allow such a thing to happen was worthy of a moment's more of my contemplation. I envy those who can retain their faith through such a loss and even imagine a purpose to it. I cannot. But still I hope for a reunion with the soul of my departed son, so what kind of Agnostic am I?

We are all burdened by memories of injury or rejection or unfairness. Sometimes we hold on to these grievances with a bitter determination that causes us to become preoccupied with the persons or institutions we hold responsible for our unhappiness.

We live in a culture in which the sense of being wronged is pervasive. If every misfortune can be blamed on someone else, we are relieved of the difficult task of examining our own contributory behavior or just accepting the reality that life is and has always been full of adversity. Most of all, by placing responsibility outside ourselves we miss out on the healing knowledge that what happens to us is not nearly as important as the attitude we adopt in response.

Some years ago, while standing in a ski lift line, I was run down by a riderless snowmobile with a frozen throttle. My injuries, while temporarily disabling, were not permanent, and it was hard for me to see this as other than an example of life's unpredictable hazards. I couldn't convince myself that the cause of snowmobile safety would be materially advanced by my collecting money from a lawsuit. The operators of the ski slope apologized and gave me some free lift tickets, and that was that. I came away from the experience with a good story and a new respect for the power of large moving objects.

Think of the slights, the insults, the rebukes, and, most important, the unfulfilled dreams that are a part of every life. Think of the ways in which our closest relationships are subject to complaint and score keeping. For most of us the process of nursing blame for past injury distracts us from the essential question of what we need to do *now* to improve our lives.

For many people the past is like an endlessly entertaining, if frequently painful, movie they replay for themselves over and over. It contains all the explanations, all the misery, all the drama that went into making us what we are today. That it may also, when checked against the versions of others who were there, be largely a work of our imagination does not detract from its power to occupy our attention. And to what end? We cannot now change the parts that we wish were different, the unfairnesses, the injuries. What is the point in holding on to our outrage and unhappiness? Do we have a choice?

Coming to terms with our past is inevitably a process of forgiveness, of letting go, the simplest and most difficult of all human endeavors. It is simultaneously an act of will and of surrender. And it often seems impossible until the moment you do it.

As a way of inducing reflection I frequently ask people

to write their own epitaphs. This exercise in summarizing their lives in a few words inevitably produces puzzlement and often results in some humorous and self-denigrating responses. Among them: "He read a lot of magazines," "She started slowly, then backed off," "I told you I was sick," and "I'm glad that's over." I encourage more thought about this and people begin to identify those aspects of their lives of which they are proud, their roles as parents, spouses, people of faith.

I actually think this exercise should be incorporated into every written will. At the point when people are contemplating their deaths, why not suggest that they add a paragraph that reads "And for my epitaph I would like the following, . . . ?" People sometimes ask me what I would choose for my own. I tell them I like the words of Raymond Carver:

> *And did you get what*
> *you wanted from this life, even so?*
> *I did.*
> *And what did you want?*
> *To call myself beloved, to feel myself*
> *beloved on the earth.*

About the Author

GORDON LIVINGSTON, M.D. is a graduate of West Point and the Johns Hopkins School of Medicine. He has been a physician since 1967. He is a psychiatrist and writer who has contributed to the *Washington Post*, the *San Francisco Chronicle*, the *Baltimore Sun* and *Reader's Digest*. Awarded the Bronze Star for valor in Vietnam, he is also the author of *Only Spring*. He lives and works in Columbia, Maryland.